THE
INVISIBLE
THREAD

I ran outside to find a place to cry, but there were people wherever I turned. I didn't want to see anybody, but there was no place to hide. There was no place to be alone—not in the latrine or the showers or anywhere in the entire camp.

After three months of communal living, I was tired of constantly seeing people and making idle conversation. All I wanted was to be alone in some quiet place and be anywhere but inside a prison camp. What I didn't know then was that getting out would mean going to a place far more cruel and unforgiving than Tanforan.

In memory of
my parents
for their unending love and grace
and
to my sister
for being my best friend

This edition is reprinted by arrangement with Simon & Schuster Books
for Young Readers, Simon & Schuster Children's Publishing Division.
Copyright © 1991 by Yoshiko Uchida

Library of Congress Cataloging in Publication Data
Uchida, Yoshiko. The invisible thread: [an autobiography] /
by Yoshiko Uchida.—1st Beech Tree ed.   p. cm.
Summary: Children's author Yoshiko Uchida describes
growing up in Berkeley, California, as a Nisei, second generation
Japanese American, and her family's internment in a Nevada
concentration camp during World War II.
1. Uchida, Yoshiko—Biography—Juvenile literature. 2. Authors,
American—20th century—Biography—Juvenile literature.
3. Japanese Americans—Social life and customs—Juvenile literature.
[1. Uchida, Yoshiko. 2. Authors, American. 3. Japanese Americans—
Social life and customs. 4. Japanese Americans—Evacuation and
relocation, 1942–1945.] I. Title. [PS3571.C247Z465 1995]
813'.54—dc20 [B] 95-14038 CIP AC
ISBN 0-688-13703-2

Originally published in 1991 by Julian Messner,
a division of Simon & Schuster.
First Beech Tree Edition, 1995.
7 9 10 8

YOSHIKO UCHIDA

THE INVISIBLE THREAD

A BEECH TREE PAPERBACK BOOK

NEW YORK

CONTENTS

THE
INVISIBLE
THREAD

1
NEVER CATCHING UP

"If you tell Mama . . . all right for you!" my sister Keiko threatens.

I haven't the vaguest idea what she means by "all right for you," but I certainly don't want to find out.

"If I catch you telling . . . all right for you!"

I don't tell. I'd never tell. Not in a million years.

Keiko is four years older than I am—a worldly ten when I am still a first-grader six. She is bold and daring. She does everything better than I do, from climbing trees, to roller skating, to playing the piano.

I think she is so smart that when she takes a piece of chewing gum from her mouth and shapes it into a fishbone, I actually believe she can lure a cat home with it.

I do everything she tells me to, like an obedient slave. If I want a new deck of playing cards, but she forbids me, I simply give up and say, "Never mind."

It takes a few more years of growing up for me to realize that she can sometimes be pretty mean, and I start fighting back. One day we have a big fight and she chases me around the house with a coat hanger. If that's what "all right for you" means, well, I decide I can live with that.

But the trouble with being a younger sister is that you can never catch up. When I am finally ten, she is already fourteen. She has learned how to dance and has talked Mama into letting her take "popular music lessons." She drives us all crazy with her endless rendition of "In a Little Gypsy Tearoom," while I am still stuck with boring "Minuet in G."

She will always be older, always ahead of me, even though I skipped half of the second grade. Still, we played together quite well. We had good times, and she eventually became, and still is, my best friend.

We grew up in a sunny three-bedroom bungalow in Berkeley, California. There was a large yard in back with two peach trees that only gave us hard green fruit. There was also a more generous apricot tree that bore so much fruit we had to call in the neighbors to help us eat it all, and a fig tree I only tolerated because it was there. We also had wild sour rhubarb and a blackberry bush that rambled over the back fence, providing endless amounts of berries for Mama's wonderful jam.

Papa was a cheerful, friendly, and confident businessman who was the assistant manager at Mitsui & Company (a Japanese import-export firm) in San Francisco. He commuted to his office across the bay each day on the ferry.

He loved being with people and spent much of his time helping anyone in need. He also loved working in our garden and grew enormous white chrysanthemums that measured fourteen inches in diameter and giant sweet peas that filled the air with their sweet scent. In our front garden he grew exotic yellow calla lilies, lavender London Smoke carnations, and prize-winning gladiolas that passersby often stopped to admire.

The flowers were mostly for Mama, a gentle, caring, reflective person who not only loved poetry and books, but just about any plant or flower that Papa could grow.

There was plenty in the backyard for Keiko and me as well. We had a large sandbox, a pair of swings that hung from a beam as high as our house, and a striped canvas hammock that Papa bought to comfort us when one of our dogs died.

Our neighbors to the left, the Harpainters, were a lovely Swiss family. Mama and Mrs. Harpainter had friendly chats over the fence as they hung out their laundry, and I walked their two young boys, Teddy and Bobby, to school. They seemed almost like relatives. So did our neighbors to the right, the Dorans, a Norwegian family whose two blond daughters, Marian and Solveig, were our best friends.

Keiko and I spent hours playing with the two girls, and in the 1930s when we were growing up, our pleasures were simple. We left notes for each other in a cigar box on the fence, we put on shows for the neighborhood kids dressed up in our Halloween costumes, we roller-skated down the block together, and often enjoyed with them the delicious root beer their father made in his basement.

Cops and robbers was one of our favorite games, and I often ended up being a robber, with my hands and feet tied up so I couldn't escape. Once when their boy cousin played with us, and was one of the cops, he commanded me to "Get over by the garage."

Of course I obeyed. The trouble was, I couldn't walk very well with my hands and feet tied up. I fell flat on my face and broke off half of my front tooth. The dentist patched it up with a pin and some cement, but after that I could never bite into a piece of chewy candy because half my tooth would then end up in the candy instead of on my tooth where it belonged.

It was one of those hardships in life I had to put up with—like braces, which came later. But I suffered most on those days when Keiko and I went to the corner store with a nickel or dime to spend on penny candy. We would sometimes spend a half hour poring over the glass containers filled with such delights as caramel chews and Tootsie Rolls and licorice and peppermint sticks. I hated having to pass up the Jujubes that stuck to every tooth, so I had to poke in a finger to scrape them off.

If we didn't come in by supper time, Mama would come out to the back porch and ring a little black bell to call us in. She always used the bell because she didn't like shouting to us. In fact, she rarely raised her voice to us and never, of course, her hand. She was a kind and tenderhearted lady.

Keiko and I were actually thrown together much more than we would have chosen to be, for we shared the same center bedroom next to the bathroom. The front bedroom was kept as a guest room for the many friends who spent the night in our home. We also shared a bureau, divided into her drawers and mine, and a closet which I felt contained, on my side, far too many hand-me-downs from Keiko.

"I'm only the Salvation Army around here," I used to grumble.

But actually Mama was an excellent seamstress and made beautiful dresses for both of us, decorated with fine tucks, smocking, hemstitching, rows of tiny mother-of-pearl buttons, and embroidery. She would embroider tiny pink roses on my petticoats so I could tell which side was the front. She made white pongee dresses with red and blue belts for us to wear to the 1932 Olympic Games in Los Angeles. And

I especially loved the voile party dresses she made (red for me and blue for Keiko) with capes that had hand-rolled hems.

Although my sister didn't like to admit it, she and I had a good deal in common. One thing we both hated with a passion was all the company that seemed to come in a never-ending stream, mostly from Japan.

Mama and Papa had both left behind a host of friends in their homeland, and it seemed that any friend of theirs, or even friends of friends, who came to America always came to see us. They came for dinner, of course, and many of them stayed overnight in our guest room.

It was as though a long invisible thread would always bind Mama and Papa to the country they had left behind. And that thread seemed to wind just as surely around Keiko and me as well.

It was like my broken tooth and the braces. It was just something I had to put up with. But I didn't like it much and wasn't above finding ways to let our guests know exactly how I felt about them.

2
OH BROOM, GET TO WORK

I was on my way home from school when I found it. A little dead sparrow. It lay still and stiff, its legs thrust in the air like two sticks. It was the first dead creature I had seen close up, and it filled me with both dread and fascination.

I knew what I would do. I would give the bird a nice funeral. Mama would find a piece of soft red silk for me from her bag of sewing scraps. I would wrap the bird in a silken shroud, put it in a candy box, and bury it beneath the peach tree. Maybe I would have Mama say a prayer for it, like the minister did at real funerals.

I picked up the bird carefully, cupping it in both hands, and ran home. I rushed through the kitchen and flung open the swinging door to the dining room.

"Look, Mama! I found a dead sparrow!"

But Mama was busy. She was sitting in the easy chair, knitting quietly. Sitting across from her on the sofa was a squat blob of a man—balding and gray—as silent as a mushroom.

The only sound was the soft ticking of the Chelsea clock on the mantel above the fireplace. I could see dust motes floating in the shaft of late afternoon sun that filtered in from the small west window.

Poor Mama was stuck with company again. She and the guest had both run out of things to say, but the visitor didn't want to leave.

"Hello, Yo Chan," my mother called. She seemed happy for the intrusion. "How was school today?"

But all I thought was, company again! It wasn't the first time a visitor had deprived me of my mother's time and attention, and I was tired of having them intrude into our lives uninvited. I stomped out of the living room without even a word of greeting to our guest, and knew I would have to bury the sparrow by myself.

Mama might have sung a Japanese hymn for me in her high, slightly off-key voice, and she certainly would have offered a better prayer than I could devise. But I did the best I could.

"Dear Heavenly Father," I began. "Please bless this little bird. It never hurt anybody. Thank you. Amen."

I buried the box beneath a mound of soft, loose dirt, picked a few nasturtiums to lay on top, and made a cross out of two small twigs.

The gray-blob mushroom was just another of the countless visitors, usually from Japan, who came to see my parents. They were both graduates of Doshisha, one of Japan's leading Christian universities, and had close ties with many of its professors. This meant that many of our visitors were ministers or young men studying to become ministers at the Pacific School of Religion in Berkeley.

Once in a while, one of the visitors would be a pleasant surprise. Like the Reverend Kimura, who sang the books of the Bible to the tune of an old folk song.

"*Mah-tai, Mah-ko, Luka, Yoha-neh-deh-un* . . ." he sang out in a loud, clear voice. "*Shito, Roma, Corinto, Zen-ko-sho* . . ." He clapped in time as he sang.

I saw Mama's eyes light up as she listened, and soon she joined in, clapping and singing and laughing at the pure joy of it.

Mama surprised me sometimes. She could be a lot of fun depending on whom she was with. It was too bad, I thought, that so much of the time she had to be serious and proper, while visiting ministers smothered her with their pious attitudes.

To me they were all achingly and endlessly boring. It was only once in a great while that a Reverend Kimura turned up, like a bright red jelly bean in a jar full of black licorice.

One pompous minister from Japan not only stayed overnight, which was bad enough, but left his dirty bathwater in the tub for Mama to wash out.

"What nerve!" Keiko fumed.

"I'll say!" I echoed.

But Mama explained that in Japan everyone washed and rinsed outside the tub and got in just to soak. "That way the water in the tub stays clean, and you leave it for the next person."

Mama got down on her knees to wash out the tub, saying, "We're lucky he didn't try to wash himself outside the tub and flood the bathroom."

Some kind of luck, I thought.

I didn't feel at all lucky about the seminary students who often dropped in, plunked themselves down on our sofa, and stayed until they were invited to have supper with us.

"Poor boys, they're lonely and homesick," Mama would say.

"They just need some of Mama's kind heart and good cooking," Papa would add. And if they needed some fatherly advice, he was more than willing to dispense plenty of that as well.

Both my parents had grown up poor, and they also knew what it was to be lonely. They cared deeply about other people and were always ready to lend a helping hand to anyone. Mama couldn't bear to think of her children ever being less than kind and caring.

"Don't ever be indifferent," she would say to Keiko and me. "That is the worst fault of all."

It was a fault she certainly never had. She would even send vitamins or herbs to some ailing person she had just met in the dentist's waiting room.

On holidays all the Japanese students from the Pacific School of Religion—sometimes as many as five or six—were invited to dinner. Keiko and I always complained shamelessly when they came.

"Aw, Mama . . . do you *have* to invite them?"

But we knew what we were expected to do. We flicked the dust cloth over the furniture, added extra boards to the dining room table so it filled up the entire room, and set it with Mama's good linen tablecloth and the company china.

If it was to be a turkey dinner, we put out the large plates and good silverware. If it was a sukiyaki dinner, we put out the rice bowls, smaller dishes, and black lacquer chopsticks.

The men came in their best clothes, their squeaky shoes shined, their hair smelling of camellia hair oil. Papa didn't cook much else, but he was an expert when it came to making sukiyaki, and he cooked it right at the table with gas piped in from the kitchen stove. As the men arrived, he would start the fat sizzling in the small iron pan.

Soon Mama would bring out huge platters laden with thin slivers of beef, slices of bean curd cake, scallions, bamboo shoots, spinach, celery, and yam noodle threads. Then

Papa would combine a little of everything in broth flavored with soy sauce, sugar, and wine, and the mouth-watering smells would drift through the entire house.

One evening in the middle of a sukiyaki dinner, one of the guests, Mr. Okada, suddenly rose from the table and hurried into the kitchen. We all stopped eating as the scholarly Mr. Okada vanished without explanation.

"Mama," I began, "he's going the wrong way if he has to . . ."

Mama stopped me with a firm hand on my knee. My sister and I looked at each other. What did he want in the kitchen anyway? More rice? Water? What?

It seemed a half hour before Mr. Okada finally reappeared. But he was smiling and seemed much happier.

"I'm sorry," he murmured, "but it was so warm I had to remove my winter undershirt." He wiped his face with a big handkerchief and added, "I feel much better now."

I knew if I looked at Keiko we would both explode. But I did. And we did. We laughed so hard we had to leave the table and rush into the kitchen holding our sides. Keiko and I often got the giggles at company dinners, and the harder we tried to stop, the harder we laughed. The only solution was for us not ever to glance at each other if we felt the giggles coming on.

In spite of all our grumbling, Keiko and I often enjoyed ourselves at these dinners. Sometimes it was Papa who provided the laughs. He loved to talk, and everyone always liked listening to his stories. Sometimes he would tell a joke he had heard at the office:

A visitor from Japan looked up at the sky. "Beautiful pigeons!" he says to a native San Franciscan.

"No, no," answers the native. "Those aren't pigeons, they're gulls."

The visitor replies, smiling, "Well, gulls or boys, they're beautiful pigeons!"

Much laughter all around.

After dinner Papa liked to gather everyone around the piano. He had a good baritone voice, often sang solos at church, and even organized the church choir. Keiko played the piano, and we sang everything from "Old Black Joe" to "In the Good Old Summertime."

Sometimes Keiko and I added to the entertainment by playing duets for our guests—a fairly audacious act since most of the time I hadn't practiced all week. It never occurred to me then, but I suppose we were just as boring to them as they so often seemed to us.

I once thought I'd found the perfect solution for getting rid of unwanted guests. Mrs. Wasa, who was like an adopted grandmother, told me one day of an old Japanese superstition.

"If you want someone to leave," she said, "just drape a cloth over the bristles of a broom and stand it upside down. It always works!"

I filed that wonderful bit of information inside my head, and the very next time Mama was trapped in the living room with another silent mushroom, I gave it a try. I did just as Mrs. Wasa instructed and stood the broom at the crack of the swinging door leading to the dining and living rooms.

"Oh broom," I murmured. "Get to work!"

I kept a watchful eye on our visitor, and before too long, he actually got up and left.

"Mama, it worked! It worked!" I shouted, dancing into the living room with the broom. "He left! I got him to leave!"

But Mama was horrified.

"*Mah*, Yo Chan," she said. "You put the broom at the doorway where he could see?"

I nodded. "I didn't think he'd notice."

Only then did I realize that our visitor had not only seen

the broom, but had probably left because he knew a few Japanese superstitions himself.

I'd always thought the seminary on the hill was bent on endlessly churning out dull ministers to try my soul. But that afternoon I felt as though I'd evened the score just a little.

3

BEING JAPANESE AMERICAN

Superstitions were not the only Japanese things in my life. A lot more of me was Japanese than I realized, whether I liked it or not.

I was born in California, recited the Pledge of Allegiance to the flag each morning at school, and loved my country as much as any other American—maybe even more.

Still, there was a large part of me that was Japanese simply because Mama and Papa had passed on to me so much of their own Japanese spirit and soul. Their own values of loyalty, honor, self-discipline, love, and respect for one's parents, teachers, and superiors were all very much a part of me.

There was also my name, which teachers couldn't seem to pronounce properly even when I shortened my first name to Yoshi. And there was my Japanese face, which closed more and more doors to me as I grew older.

How wonderful it would be, I used to think, if I had blond hair and blue eyes like Marian and Solveig. Or a name like Mary Anne Brown or Betty Johnson.

If only I didn't have to ask such questions as, "Can we come swim in your pool? We're Japanese." Or when we were looking for a house, "Will the neighbors object if we move in next door?" Or when I went for my first professional haircut, "Do you cut Japanese hair?"

Still, I didn't truly realize how different I was until the summer I was eleven. Although Papa usually went on business trips alone, bringing back such gifts as silver pins for Mama or charm bracelets for Keiko and me, that summer he was able to take us along, thanks to a railroad pass.

We took the train, stopping at the Grand Canyon, Houston, New Orleans, Washington, D.C., New York, Boston, Niagara Falls, and on the way home, Chicago, to see the World's Fair.

Crossing the Mississippi River was a major event, as our train rolled onto a barge and sailed slowly over that grand body of water. We all got off the train for a closer look, and I was so impressed with the river's majesty, I felt impelled to make some kind of connection with it. Finally, I leaned over the barge rail and spit so a part of me would be in the river forever.

For my mother, the high point of the trip was a visit to the small village of Cornwall, Connecticut. There she had her first meeting with the two white American pen pals with whom she had corresponded since her days at Doshisha University. She also visited one of her former missionary teachers, Louise DeForest, who had retired there. And it was there I met a young girl my age, named Cathy Sellew. We became good friends, corresponded for many years, and met again as adults when I needed a home and a friend.

Everyone in the village greeted us warmly, and my father

was asked to say a few words to the children of the Summer Vacation Church School—which he did with great relish.

Most of the villagers had never before met a Japanese American. One smiling woman shook my hand and said, "My, but you speak English so beautifully." She had meant to compliment me, but I was so astonished, I didn't know what to say. I realized she had seen only my outer self—my Japanese face—and addressed me as a foreigner. I knew then that I would always be different, even though I wanted so badly to be like my white American friends.

I hated having Mama stop on the street and greet a friend with a series of bows as was customary in Japan. "Come on, Mama," I would say impatiently tugging at her sleeve. I felt as though everyone was staring at us.

I was humiliated when the post office called us one Sunday requesting that we pick up immediately a package of rotting food. Actually, it was just some pungent pickled *daikon* (long white radish), sent by a friend who knew Papa loved eating it with rice and hot tea. But the man at the post office thrust it at us at arm's length, as though it were a piece of stinking garbage.

Keiko and I absolutely refused when Mama wanted us to learn how to read and write Japanese. We wanted to be *Americans*, not Japanese!

"Wouldn't it be nice to write to your grandmother in Japanese?" she asked.

"It's easier if you write her, Mama," we said.

"Don't you want to be able to read those nice storybooks from Japan?"

We didn't. Not really. We liked having Mama read them to us. We read our own favorites in English.

I loved going to the South Berkeley branch of the public library, where I would head for the children's corner. There

I looked for the books with stars on their spines, which meant they were mysteries. I read such books as Augusta H. Seaman's *The Boarded Up House* and *The Mystery of the Old Violin*. I also liked Hugh Lofting's *Dr. Doolittle* books, and loved Louisa May Alcott's *Little Women* and *Little Men*. Other favorites were Anna Sewell's *Black Beauty* and Frances Hodgson Burnett's *The Secret Garden*.

Learning Japanese, Keiko and I felt, would only make us seem more different from our white classmates. So Mama didn't force us to go to Japanese Language School after regular school, as many of our Nisei (second-generation Japanese) friends did.

We finally agreed, however, to let her teach us Japanese during summer vacations when she also taught us how to embroider. We loved learning how to make daisies and rosebuds on pillowcases, but we certainly didn't make it easy for Mama to teach us Japanese. Keiko and I grumbled endlessly as we tried to learn how to read and write the complicated Japanese characters, and by the time each summer rolled around, we had forgotten most of what we had learned the year before.

Still, we managed to learn a lot of Japanese by osmosis. Our parents spoke Japanese to each other and to us, although we usually answered in English, sprinkling in a few Japanese words here and there.

Then there were many Japanese phrases we used every day. We always said, *"Itadaki masu,"* before each meal, and *"Gochiso sama"* afterward to thank Mama for preparing the food. The first thing we called out when we came home from school was *"Tadaima!* I'm home!"

The Japanese names Mama gave to the tools and implements around the house were the sounds they made. The vacuum cleaner was the *buhn-buhn*. The carpet sweeper was the *goro-goro*. Mama's little sewing scissors with the silver bell tied to it was the *chirin-chirin*.

Keiko and I often talked in a strange hybrid language. "It's your turn to do the *goro-goro* today." Or, "Mama said to *buhn-buhn* the living room." And anytime Mama asked us to fetch the *chirin-chirin,* we knew exactly what she meant.

Every night when we were little, Keiko and I would climb into bed and wait for Mama to come sit between our two beds and read a Japanese story to us. I first heard such wonderful folktales as "The Old Man Who Made the Flowers Bloom" and "The Tongue-Cut Sparrow" from her.

Although Papa loved to sing American folk songs, he and Mama taught us many Japanese songs that still float through my memory today. Their prayers, too, were always in Japanese—Papa's grace before meals (nice and short) and Mama's prayers at bedtime (not so short). So when it came to praying, I always did it in Japanese, even after I grew up.

We always celebrated Dolls Festival Day on March 3, as all girls did in Japan, displaying special dolls for the occasion. Mama would open the big brown trunk in the basement and bring up dozens of tiny wooden boxes containing her Japanese doll collection. These were not dolls to be played with, but to be treasured carefully and viewed only once a year.

A formal festival doll set consisted of an emperor and empress presiding over their court of musicians, guards, ladies-in-waiting, and so forth down to the lowliest member of the imperial court.

But Mama's collection was different. She did have an emperor and empress, but the rest were tiny dolls or toys that had caught her fancy. There were good-luck charms on ivory rings, round-bottomed *daruma* dolls that always sprang up when pushed down, miniature tea sets and kitchen utensils, dolls that were characters from folktales or dolls she'd dressed herself as a child, balls made of colored silk thread, small clay bells from old temples, folk toy animals that brought good luck, and anything else Mama wanted to include. It was all sort of a pleasant, Mama-like jumble laid out on a table covered with a festive red felt cloth.

"Bring out your own dolls, too," she would tell us. "We don't want them to feel left out."

So Keiko and I would bring out our white baby dolls with brown hair and green glass eyes and place them around the table as well.

Until I was much older and wiser, the Japanese dolls didn't mean much to me. Mama seemed to enjoy them more than Keiko or I did, and she would often have friends to tea to share her pleasure in their yearly appearance.

As for me, it was my white baby doll and my Patsy doll that I loved, even though they didn't look anything like me. I suppose it was because I always thought of myself as being an American. I just didn't realize how much of me was Japanese as well.

4
OUR
JAPANESE
SUNDAYS

On Sundays we were the most Japanese of all, for we spent a good part of our day at the small Japanese church in Oakland where we went each week, rain or shine.

Actually, Mama's Sunday tasks began the night before. On Saturday nights she prepared food for the Sunday picnics or dinners to which she would invite a variety of students or bachelors with no place to go.

Keiko and I often went to sleep with the sound of her knife chattering on the cutting board and the tantalizing smell of chicken bubbling in soy sauce and sugar drifting into our bedroom.

Sunday mornings, while Keiko and I had our toast and hot cocoa in our Orphan Annie mugs, Mama cooked a big pot of rice. When it was done, she wrapped it up in the heavy quilt at the foot of her bed to keep warm until we got home from church.

Some Sundays we took everything—the lunch and the company—to Lake Merritt for a picnic. We would spread the car blanket on the grass and have rice balls and teriyaki chicken on little red lacquer dishes, using black lacquer chopsticks.

As passersby stared, I would cringe, hoping they didn't notice our unusual picnic fare. Still, Mama's Japanese food was so good, I would have chosen it over baloney sand-wiches any day.

We left home early on Sunday mornings so Papa could make stops along the way to pick up children for Sunday School. For many years he was its superintendent, and Mama was one of its teachers, so we had to be on time.

Mama was also president of the Women's Society, and took it upon herself to bring home the soiled roller towel from the church restroom each week, wash it, and take in a clean one. She also made booties for each new baby born into the church, and undoubtedly did many more things of which I was unaware.

We children gathered first in the dark high-ceilinged chapel to hear a Bible story and sing some hymns before di-viding up into classes. In winter it was so cold, we huddled around the small floor grilles trying to warm our feet with the faint wisps of heat from the coal furnace before taking our seats to sing "Jesus Loves Me." Sometimes we would even see our breath in the icy cold air.

My class met in an old wooden building behind the chapel that we called "The Back House." It was a dilapi-dated structure that once housed bachelors who couldn't yet afford to send for brides from Japan. Its sole occupant then, however, was Mr. Toga, a grouchy, shrill-voiced old bachelor who rattled about upstairs all alone.

I heard all sorts of tales about Mr. Toga and believed them all. He was so miserly, it was said, that he would walk ten miles to Berkeley rather than spend a nickel on streetcar fare. He saved on soap, they said, by drying his handkerchiefs on the stove instead of washing them. And he had never married, people said, because the love of his life had died.

He was quick to scold anyone who displeased him, including a succession of long-winded ministers who came to our little church. I think he struck terror into many of their hearts as he sat grim-faced, arms folded across his chest, showing his contempt for their sermons. And if the closing hymn droned on too long, he simply stood up, raised his hand, and said, "Enough! I have an announcement to make!"

The singing would come to a sudden halt. The startled organist would stop pumping the pedals of the wheezing reed organ, and it would wind down like a deflating balloon, leaving half-finished notes dangling in the air. Then Mr. Toga would make whatever announcement he wished to make.

One loud shout and a wave of the hand from Mr. Toga could make even the big boys stop throwing pebbles at the goldfish in the slimy green pond behind the church. When Mr. Toga came marching down the steps of The Back House, everyone got out of the way, as though a king were approaching.

I guess Papa was about the only one who was any match for Mr. Toga. They had become friends when my parents first joined the church, and I grew up calling him "Tonton." Mama often invited him for lunch on Sundays, and Keiko and I would get the giggles over his clicking false teeth.

"He's got talking teeth," we would tell our amazed friends.

"Honest? What do they say?"

"In English or in Japanese?"

"English! What do they say?"

If we felt silly enough, we might sing, "Clickety-cluck-alunk-alunk, the teeth are talking ka-chunk ka-chunk . . ."

"Aw, go on!"

Now that I think about it, those ill-fitting teeth might well have been responsible for his crabby disposition. And if they were, I guess I should be grateful to them, because the fearsome Mr. Toga has appeared as a character in several of my books and short stories. So have many of those visitors I found so dull and boring.

For me the worst part of Sundays was the long wait for my parents, as they and the other Issei (first-generation Japanese) attended the Japanese service. It often lasted well over an hour, and it was our dreary lot to entertain ourselves until we could go home and have lunch.

Even after the service ended, Papa stayed to count the offering and lock up the building. I often thought he acted more like a minister than the minister himself.

Sometimes Keiko and I would sit in the backseat of our car and read mystery books while we waited. Sometimes we would play marbles with the other waiting children. And sometimes we would just be wicked and toss pebbles into the fish pond since we knew Mr. Toga was safely tucked away in the chapel.

As it grew close to twelve-thirty, my sister would often say, "Go see if they're done yet." Always her obedient slave, I would tiptoe to the back of the chapel, peer through the crack at the door, and inspect the meager congregation.

The men sat to the left of the center aisle and the women to the right. All of them were dressed in their black Sunday clothes, looking somber and weary. Some seemed to be dozing, their heads slumped over their chests. But Mr. Toga usually sat as straight and rigid as a telephone pole.

Many times the minister seemed to be scolding the congregation, and I wondered what these gentle people had done to make him shout at them like that. I knew they were good folk. Most of the men struggled for survival during the Depression. They operated dry cleaners, or grocery stores, or shoe repair shops, or laundries, and did not have an easy time in a country that would not allow them to become citizens or to own land.

Some of their wives did housework for white families who lived up in the hills. Others helped their husbands, working beside them all day, then cooking and caring for their families in the evenings.

Life was hard for all of them, and I thought the minister was mean to scold them on their one day of rest and quiet. But they put up with his wrath in the same stoic way in which they bore all of life's burdens.

Mama and Papa understood their burdens and always listened to their troubles, helping them when they could. Because Papa was a salaried man at Mitsui & Company, he did not have the worries of a small shopkeeper. We were lucky not to feel the full brunt of the Depression as they did, but my parents were always frugal and never indulged in luxuries.

Papa never failed to dispense advice or money to anyone who asked for help, and Mama often baked cakes and dozens of cream puffs to provide comfort of a different kind.

I believe they both had a generosity of spirit that caused them to care deeply about the struggles of their fellow men because they never forgot the harsh memories of their own youth in Japan.

5

IKU
AND
TAKASHI

It was October 1916. My mother, Iku Umegaki, aged twenty-four, stood shivering on the deck of a small ship, watching the dim outlines of Japan fade into the distance. Her eyes were red and swollen from weeping, and her throat ached with loneliness.

"I'll be back, Oka San," she whispered to her mother. "I'll be back someday with my husband. Wait for me."

Iku was leaving behind her widowed mother, three younger brothers, and a sister. Her father, once a samurai (feudal warrior who observed a special code of honor), and then a prefectural governor, had died when she was twelve. Ever since, life had been a difficult struggle for the Umegaki family. Unable to feed all her children, her mother had taken her youngest son to a Buddhist temple to be raised as a priest.

Iku's mother earned money by sewing, and was counting on her eldest daughter to help out when she finished high school. Still, when Iku told her that she wanted to go on to college, her mother allowed her to enter Doshisha University at a time when very few women even thought of pursuing a higher education.

Iku worked for three women missionary teachers in return for her room, board, and tuition, and enrolled in the Department of English. In those days Doshisha was a small college, where students and professors became good friends in a close, caring community.

Iku so admired and respected two of her teachers, Louise DeForest and Ellen Emerson Cary, that they remained close friends for the rest of her life. She ran errands for them and spent many hours on such chores as hemming their long, full skirts or polishing their shoes. They in turn gave her a lifelong love for English literature.

Now, a year after completing her education and teaching English to factory workers in Kyoto for a time, Iku had decided to leave behind everything she held dear and marry a man she had not yet met.

She knew that Dwight Takashi Uchida had immigrated to the United States in 1906 to join his mother and a married sister in Seattle, Washington. She knew he was fast becoming a successful businessman.

But it was not for these reasons she had decided to begin a new life with the man who was to become my father. It was because in those days it was the custom for all marriages to be arranged formally by go-betweens, and she completely trusted and respected the Doshisha professors who recommended their union.

The president of Doshisha University himself had introduced Takashi Uchida to her. And Dr. Dwight W. Learned, a distinguished missionary professor, had thought so highly of Takashi that he had given him his own name, Dwight. Both men were glowing in their praise for the bright, enterprising young man in Seattle, and for Iku that was enough.

She had searched her heart and soul carefully and decided to correspond with Takashi. After exchanging letters and photographs for over a year, Iku finally made her decision. By then she knew that Takashi was a good man, and she decided at last to take the giant leap across the Pacific Ocean. She was ready to become the wife of Dwight Takashi Uchida.

A shy, studious young woman, Iku loved to read and to write poetry. In her steamer trunk she brought with her the volumes of Alfred, Lord Tennyson, Henry Wadsworth Longfellow, Robert Browning, George Eliot, and Samuel Johnson. She had labored over them in college and their margins were filled with the notes she had scribbled in Japanese.

Her missionary teachers had prepared her well, she thought. And she hoped she would be able to speak and understand the language of this strange new country to which she now journeyed.

As the small ship slowly approached the shores of America, she was relieved to feel a sense of hope and joy edge in beside the great loneliness and fear that filled her heart.

In America, Dwight Takashi Uchida had worked hard for ten years before he could think about marriage. He was energetic and capable, and after only one year at the Furuya General Merchandise Store in Seattle, he was appointed manager of its Portland branch. Soon it became the most successful of the ten Furuya stores. It doubled in size, and in addition to selling dry goods and food supplies, it housed a branch of the U.S. Post Office, proudly flying an American flag from its rooftop.

As a Furuya employee, Takashi always wore an immaculate white shirt and a black bow tie. He was trained to be punctual, never to let the telephone ring more than twice, and to be unfailingly courteous to all his customers.

"You never know," Mr. Furuya warned, "when you may someday find yourself indebted to the humblest of your customers."

Takashi never forgot his mentor's advice, and retained the Furuya qualities for the rest of his life—even wearing the white shirt and black bow tie every day.

Takashi was used to hard work. His father, a samurai turned teacher, had died when he was ten. His mother had gathered her five children together then and told them she could not care for them alone.

"I must send each of you to live with a relative," she explained. "Be good children, and I promise we will all be together again someday."

So it was that Takashi left his mother and four sisters and went to live with an uncle, trudging in straw sandals for more than six miles to his new home.

In the meantime, his mother went to Kyoto to work as a maid in the home of the missionaries Dr. and Mrs. Dwight W. Learned of Doshisha University. She worked hard, became a Christian, and after a few years was able to call her children to her side, one by one.

Reunited with his family in Kyoto, Takashi worked for a year in a doctor's office. Then delivering milk in the mornings and working nights as a telephone operator, he attended Doshisha University, completing the regular five-year course of study in four years.

Ready for new adventures, he sailed for Hawaii to become a Japanese Language School teacher. He earned $25 a month, sent half of it home to help his sisters through college, and earned extra money by reading the Bible to a wealthy white widow on Sundays.

He left for California in 1906, arriving in San Francisco two months after the big earthquake that had devastated the city. The tower of the Ferry Building was still askew and Market Street was piled high with ash.

Instead of going on to Yale to study medicine as he had hoped, he joined his mother and sister in Seattle. Working at Furuya's, he saved enough money to call his remaining sisters from Japan. That accomplished, he was ready at last to settle down. And so it was that he wrote to Iku Umegaki, asking her to join him in America.

They were married in Portland, Oregon, in 1917 and moved soon after to California, where Takashi was invited to join the San Francisco branch of Mitsui & Company. They made their first home in Oakland, California, where my sister, Keiko, was born, and I was born in Alameda four years later.

My studious, dreamer mother was so different from my brisk, energetic businessman father. They were total opposites, and yet they complemented each other well. My mother nourished the tenderness in my father that Keiko and I always felt, and eventually, he even tried his hand at writing poetry. He also grew to love flowers as much as she did.

He often came in from the garden, grimy with dirt, bringing Mama one of her favorite London Smoke carnations. "Here, Mama," he would say, "I dedicate this to you!"

And she would answer with a smile, "Thank you, Papa San," and put the flower in her best crystal bud vase.

Their marriage may have been an arranged one, but I have always felt that the Doshisha professors who engineered it must have been enormously proud of its great success.

6

DISCOVERING THE MAGIC

"Mama, can't we get a puppy? Please?"

"Please, Mama, can't we?"

Keiko and I begged shamelessly and finally wore Mama down. When a five-month-old collie puppy finally came into our lives, we named him Brownie. I was so excited, I simply had to do something to hold on to the magical happiness so it would never fade away.

That was when I remembered the booklet with blank pages I'd made at school. It was covered with silver and gold Christmas wrapping paper and was so special I hadn't known what to do with it. All I had written in it so far was my name and address and the word *private*.

Now at last I'd discovered a perfect use for it. I kept in it an account of everything Brownie did, from the day he was scratched by a cat, to the time he ate the rind of half a cantaloupe and his poor belly expanded to the size of a full melon. I recorded the day he learned to raise his leg at a tree and also the tragic day he came down with distemper.

Our neighbor, who was a Christian Scientist and believed in spiritual healing, came to pray for Brownie. "Mrs. Harpainter is taking care of him and is doing Christian Science," I wrote in my booklet. I truly believed she could heal him, but he was too sick to be saved and had to be put to sleep.

Nothing I truly loved had died before. Keiko and I cried so much, refusing even to go outside to play, that Papa finally bought a hammock to console us. He hung it in the backyard between the peach and the apricot trees and told us to try it out.

I lay on the striped canvas hammock, gently swaying to and fro. I looked up between the mass of green leaves at the cloudless blue sky, but all I could see were Brownie's sad eyes as we left him at the vet's. I was too desolate and devastated to enjoy the hammock. I decided then that I would do something for Brownie in my special booklet.

I used a whole page to draw a tombstone for him bearing the words *Died March 16, 1932. Ten months old.* Then, using my crayons, I surrounded the tombstone with four magnificent floral wreaths and bouquets of flowers, similar to those I had seen at the cemetery. I also drew him a tree. I thought he would like that.

When I finished, I felt better. I had found a way to give Brownie a proper ending to his brief life. I had also discovered that writing in the booklet was a means, not only of holding on to the special magic of joyous moments, but of finding comfort and solace from pain as well. It was a means of creating a better ending than was sometimes possible in real life. I had discovered what writing was all about.

Fortunately, I was able to write about other happier moments as well. There was the glorious day we got another dog—a beautiful Scotch collie we named Laddie. And the day we got our first refrigerator, enabling us to enjoy the luxury of making our own ice and even ice cream.

The refrigerator was a special boon for me because I no longer had the odious chore of emptying the pan under the ice box where water from the melting ice collected. I was also relieved of the task of hanging the sign in our window to tell the ice man how many pounds of ice we needed each day.

When my booklet was filled, I began a black leather three-ring binder notebook that I called "My Diary of Important Events." My first entry was about our sixth-grade graduation party at school. I was so impressed by the vanilla ice cream with a green Christmas tree center that I illustrated the page with a colored drawing of it.

One day when I was in the sixth grade, my favorite teacher, Miss Wolfard, put up several intriguing pictures taken from magazine covers. One was of an aproned woman watering geraniums in her window box. Another showed a boy delivering newspapers with his golden retriever. There was also a man wearing a green eyeshade and black sleeve protectors bent over a desk. There were several other pictures as well.

"Who do you think these people are?" she asked. "What's happening in their lives? See if you can write a story about one of them."

My head began to buzz with ideas, and I could hardly wait to get started. That might well have been the day I discovered how much fun it was to write stories of my own. Soon I was writing short stories in little booklets, and because like my parents, I was also frugal, I made them out of brown wrapping paper.

My first attempt was called "Jimmy Chipmunk and His

Friends—a Short Story for Small Children." The back cover read "by Yoshi Uchida, Age Ten, Low Sixth Grade." My next story was called "Willie, the Squirrel."

Two years later I allowed myself to advance to white typing paper, and using my father's typewriter, I wrote and illustrated a seven-chapter book called "Sally Jane Waters."

It never in my wildest dreams occurred to me to write about a Japanese American child, which may seem strange today. But the books I was reading at the time were only about white children and were written by white authors. The best world, it seemed to me then, was the white American world. So that was what I wrote about.

The written word was always important in our family, and I was surrounded by books. Papa bought us a complete set of *The Book of Knowledge,* a sort of junior encyclopedia, and Mama also bought many books for us, as well as for herself.

One corner of her bureau was usually piled high with magazines and books that she hoped someday to read. But unfortunately, she never found the time, and the unwieldy pile continued to grow, spilling over onto any nearby table or shelf.

Mama also kept a diary. She filled up dozens of small brown-leather five-year diaries with golden clasps to record our daily doings. But I never liked those cramped pages that forced you to squeeze a whole day into a tiny one-inch space. Instead of a daily entry, I liked to wait for a special event and fill up a whole page or more with the full glory of it.

When Mama had a few free moments, she often sat at the table in the breakfast nook, pushed aside the books, magazines, and papers spread out on it, and scribbled her poems on bits of scrap paper or the backs of old envelopes. It was as though she felt her poems were not worthy of a nice clean page in a notebook and that she could only indulge in writing them after completing her tasks as a mother and wife.

The poems she wrote were the thirty-one-syllable Japanese *tanka* and were published every other week in a small publication put out by our good friend, Mrs. Wasa.

I had a great interest in Mrs. Wasa as well, but for entirely different reasons. She seemed more of a grandmother to me than my real grandmother, and because she lived only two blocks from us, I visited her often.

I usually found her in the sunny kitchen, wearing an apron that seemed to swallow up her tiny person, daintily licking her fingers as she baked custard or a vanilla sponge cake.

"Ah, Yo Chan, you are just in time for a little taste," she would say, making me a cup of hot cocoa to go with it.

I always thought I was incredibly lucky to arrive each day at exactly the right moment, but she no doubt thoughtfully timed her baking to gladden my heart on those after-school visits.

Poetry and diary entries certainly were not the primary items of writing in our house. Both my parents were avid letter writers, communicating not only with friends and relatives in Japan, but with many friends scattered across the United States.

Of course all these people wrote back, so our mailbox was always bulging, and the mailman was a good friend. He made two deliveries each day and always had something for us in his big leather pouch.

Besides writing letters, my father kept all our financial records. His fingers could make the beads of the abacus dance in lively rhythm as he checked bills and maintained our household accounts. He wrote all the checks in the neat flowing script he had learned at night school and never left an unpaid bill on his desk for more than two days.

He liked to read, too, but his taste was quite different

from Mama's. He liked reading such magazines as *The Literary Digest, The Christian Century,* and *National Geographic,* and he never left for the office without a copy of the *San Francisco Chronicle* to read on the ferry.

Because there were no baby-sitters in the world of my childhood, our parents took us everywhere they went—to church, to the movies, to visit friends, to San Francisco's art museums (because Mama loved art), and to concerts (because Papa loved music).

My diary was filled with such entries as "Tonight we went to hear the Cossacks Chorus. They were keen!" Or "to hear Roland Hayes sing." Or "to hear Ignace Jan Paderewski play the piano." Or "to see 'The Merry Widow' " or "A Midsummer Night's Dream" or "Mme Butterfly." All of which I could only describe as "perfect!" or "swell" or "just keen!"

When I was writing about a concert or a play, one page of my diary was quite sufficient, even including an illustration. But when we went on summer trips to Los Angeles to visit my grandmother, or to Livingston to visit friends on a farm, I needed at least three pages. And my limited vocabulary of "keen" and "swell" suddenly began to seem woefully inadequate.

7

TUB UNDER THE STARS

Papa was a terrible driver. He had taught himself how to drive, and nobody had ever told him to look in both directions before driving through an intersection. Usually he looked one way, and if nothing was coming, he sailed right through with his usual buoyant confidence.

One Sunday afternoon, after we'd taken a friend of Mama's for a drive, Papa made that mistake once too often. Just two blocks from home, Papa came to a corner, looked to the left, and kept going. Unfortunately, another car was coming from the right. And that's when it happened.

We were hit broadside, and our bulky Buick simply toppled over and lay on its side like a beached whale.

Drowsing in the backseat, I was suddenly jolted on top of Mama and proceeded to scream at the top of my lungs.

Papa somehow managed to get through the window and pulled the rest of us out.

"Are you all right?" he asked each of us.

"Yes, Papa," we answered feebly. And we emerged one by one, to the astonishment of the onlookers who, having heard my screams, probably expected me at least to have a broken arm or leg.

Fortunately, we suffered only minor bumps, cuts, and bruises, and although a bit wobbly, we were able to walk home.

For me the accident was a major event worthy of an illustrated page in my diary, but Papa brushed it aside as a minor inconvenience and kept right on driving as he always had.

One summer he drove us to Livingston to visit Mr. and Mrs. Okubo. They were among the early Japanese Christian families who had settled there, tamed the dry windblown earth, and coaxed grapes to flourish where nothing had grown before. I could hardly wait to spend a few days on a real farm, for I was a child of the city who walked on sidewalks and knew only dogs and cats.

Mama was always nervous about Papa's driving, but after the accident, she was even more so. She usually sat in the back with me, often reaching out to grab my arm whenever Papa went too fast or got too close to a streetcar.

"Be careful, Papa San," she would call out. "You're going too fast." But I don't think Papa ever listened.

Keiko usually sat in front with him because she wanted to watch his every move. Already she had a fairly good idea of how to drive and was dying to get behind the wheel. In a weak moment Papa had said that maybe she could when we got out into the countryside.

As we turned off the main highway, it seemed as though

we were driving through a vast ocean of vineyards that spread out on both sides of the dusty road. Before long we could see the Okubo water pump windmill sprouting up among the grapevines.

"There it is!" Keiko shouted. "There's the Okubo farm!"

She reminded Papa of his earlier promise and convinced him there was nothing on the deserted road that she could possibly hit. Papa knew he would never hear the end of it if he didn't give her a chance, so he stopped the car.

Keiko was in heaven as Papa let her slide over behind the wheel. But poor Mama was clutching my arm again.

"Careful, Kei Chan," she cautioned. "Be careful."

Keiko started slowly, like a tired turtle. But by the time she made the final turn toward the farm, she was feeling confident and picking up a little speed.

"Honk the horn to let them know we're here," Papa said.

At which point Keiko not only honked the horn, but simultaneously crashed into Jick's dog house, knocked it over on its side, and stopped just inches short of the walnut tree.

"Look out, for heaven's sake," we all shouted. "Look out!"

Jick barked furiously at the sudden assault on his territory, and the chickens scrambled in every direction, screeching and cackling as though the end of the world had come.

The startled Okubos rushed from their house, blinking in the sun, surveying with alarm what only moments before had been their peaceful yard.

"We're here!" Keiko shouted, as if they needed to be told. "We're here!"

Because the Okubos' two grown daughters had already left home, they welcomed my sister and me as though we were their grandchildren, and we called them Oji San (uncle) and Oba San (auntie).

Oji San gave us a quick tour of the farm. He showed us

how to pump water from the well and put our heads down to gulp the cold water that came gushing out. He pointed to the outhouse, saying, "I guess you've never used one of those before." We certainly hadn't. Whenever I had to use it, I held my breath and got out as fast as I could.

He also let us look for eggs in the henhouse, and took us to the barn where we staggered about in the hayloft, trying to pitch hay with forks that were bigger than we were.

He saved the best for last, taking us to a fenced enclosure where two dusty mules ambled over to greet us.

"Meet Tom and Jerry," he said. Then pulling some scraggly weeds by the fence, he told us to feed them to the mules.

I thrust some weeds at them and the mules grabbed them hungrily, showing their enormous yellow teeth. They seemed friendly enough, but I was rather glad they were on the other side of the fence.

"They like you," Oji San said. "Maybe they'll do something nice for you later on."

"Like what, Oji San?"

Oji San just grinned and smashed his felt hat down over his forehead. "You'll see," he said. "Wait and see."

Sitting on mats spread out under the walnut tree, we had a wonderful picnic supper of soy-drenched chicken and corn grilled over an outdoor pit. There were rice balls, too, sprinkled with black sesame seeds that looked like tiny ants.

Oji San waited until the sun had dipped down behind the dusty grapevines and a soft dusky haze settled in the air. Then he announced he was taking us all on a moonlight ride through the vineyards. It was more than we'd ever hoped for.

Keiko took her usual place up front by Oji San, hoping for a brief chance at the reins. Mama and Papa chatted quietly with Oba San, and I lay stretched out in back, looking up at the enormous night sky.

There seemed to be millions and billions of stars up there.

More than I'd ever imagined existed in the universe. They seemed brighter and closer than they were in Berkeley. It was as though the entire sky had dropped closer to earth to spread out its full glory right there in front of me.

I listened to the slow *clop-clop* of the mules as they plodded through the fields, probably wondering why they were pulling a wagonload of people in the dark, instead of hauling boxes of grapes to the shed under the hot, dry sun.

I could hear crickets singing and frogs croaking and all the other gentle night sounds of the country. I felt as though I were in another more immense, never-ending world, and wished I could keep riding forever to the ends of the earth.

When we got back to the farm, it was time for an outdoor Japanese bath. Oji San built a fire under a square tin tub filled with water, banking the fire when the water was hot and inserting a wooden float so we wouldn't burn our feet or backsides when we got in.

Oba San hung some sheets on ropes strung around the tub and called out, "*Sah, ofuro!* Come, Kei Chan, Yo Chan. The bath is ready. You girls go first."

Mama gave us careful instructions about proper bathing procedures. "Wash and rinse yourselves outside before you get into the tub," she reminded us. "And keep the water clean."

When we were ready to climb in, I saw steam rising from the water and was afraid I'd be boiled alive. "You go first," I told my sister.

As always, Keiko was fearless. She jumped right in and sank down in the steaming water up to her neck.

"Ooooooh, this feels wonderful!" she said.

I quickly squeezed in next to her, and we let the warm water gurgle up to our chins.

Keiko looked up at the glorious night sky and sighed, "I could stay here forever."

"Where? In the tub?"

39

"No, silly. In Livingston, of course."

Long after I came home, I remembered Livingston, not as the small dusty farm it was, but as a magical place.

Even now, when I close my eyes, I can see the smiling, sun-browned faces of Oji San and Oba San welcoming us to their farm. I can hear our watery giggles in the steaming outdoor tub, and I can hear the small quiet songs of the creatures in the fields.

But most of all I remember the wagon ride and see again that night sky exploding with stars. It is like a beautiful speckled stone I can take from the pocket of my memory to look at over and over, remembering again the sweet peace of that little farm.

I have written about it in several of my books and stories, and the memory of it even now brings a rush of joy to my heart.

8

OBAH SAN AND MY COUSINS

Sometimes, after a stop at Livingston, Papa drove on down to Los Angeles to visit Grandma. (We called her Obah San.) But usually we took the Southern Pacific overnight sleeper on New Year's Eve, arriving just in time to celebrate New Year's with Obah San, my aunt and uncle, and six cousins.

My father's railroad pass enabled us to travel in a cozy compartment, and I loved lying in the snug upper bunk listening to the click of the wheels and the *ding-ding-ding* of the signal lights rushing by.

In the morning we went to the dining car, sparkling with fresh linens, china, and flowers, where gracious white-coated waiters treated me with the same courtesy they accorded the adults.

As the train neared Union Station, our porter came to

brush us off with his little whisk broom, and I knew I would soon see my uncle and cousins smiling and waving to us from the station platform.

Long before I got that far, however, I often came down with a fever. I was not a healthy child. I got carsick and seasick. I had knee aches (Mama called them "growing pains"), and often went to bed with a hot water bottle puffed up like a football because I'd forgotten to let the air out after pouring in the hot water. I also had nosebleeds that seemed to last for hours and a variety of unexplained fevers.

Mama could sometimes relieve my knee aches with the warmth of her "healing hands," but otherwise she resorted to medicine from Japan. Her best cure-alls were the tiny seedlike pills we called Kinbon San, but they didn't always rid me of my pre-New Year's fevers.

Although I really wanted to go to Los Angeles, I was also a bit anxious about being there. It was bad enough being intimidated by an older sister at home, but in Los Angeles I was the youngest of all thirteen of us gathered there. Most of the time I felt inadequate, and sometimes didn't dare open my mouth.

The two youngest girls were only a year or two older than I was, but they were prettier, and I thought more sophisticated, and I was often in awe of them.

They taught us how to sing such songs as "Walking My Baby Back Home," and they knew how to dance when I was still perfecting my roller skating techniques. They also did such daring things as taking us downtown to see two movies, one right after the other.

To me movies were a special treat to be indulged in only occasionally. To walk out of one theater and march right into another was a thrilling feat Keiko and I never would have attempted back home.

I always looked forward to New Year's Day, for it was a festive occasion that began with a traditional Japanese New Year's feast. We all gathered around the extended dining room table, with a bright red broiled lobster, symbol of long life, dominating its center.

Surrounding it were tiered lacquer boxes and large platters full of such delicacies as sesame *daikon* salad, herring roe, knotted seaweed, teriyaki chicken, bamboo shoots, taro, burdock and lotus root, sweet black beans, and hard-boiled eggs cut into fancy shapes.

I sampled everything except the herring roe, which I always passed up, for each dish was symbolic of long life, prosperity, or good health, and I wanted to have all those things.

I knew Obah San and my cousins had labored hard for several days preparing the feast. The family had also cleaned house, paid all the bills, and tied up loose ends, for New Year's Day was considered a time for new beginnings unsullied by the old year's debts and obligations.

"Happy New Year, Obah San! Happy New Year everybody!"

The room was filled with happy chatter as we began with traditional toasted rice cakes floating in kelp broth and then progressed to all the other delicacies.

When at last we had eaten our fill, we children drifted away from the table to go outside or to play cards or otherwise entertain ourselves.

One year one of my older cousins taught us new words to the Toreador Song from the opera *Carmen*. "Dorie, oh, Dora," he sang in his sweet tenor voice, "don't spit on the floor-ah. Spit in the spit bowl, that's what it's for-ah . . ." After that, I could never listen to *Carmen* without hearing those words.

Keiko and I loved being part of that big lively family of

six children who obligingly doubled up to accommodate us.

Because my aunt was not well, Obah San was the central figure of the household. Every morning she was the first one up, and I would find her sitting beside the stove, toasting a dozen pieces of bread at a time in the broiler. She liked to eat her toast with a thick layer of peanut butter on it, and I always believed that was what kept her healthy and well for over ninety years.

Whenever Obah San had a few spare minutes, I would see her reading her Japanese Bible, sounding out the words silently, just as she did when she prayed. God was her best friend, and each night she talked to Him for a half hour. Sitting on her bed, her legs folded beneath her, she rocked back and forth, her eyes shut tight, pouring out her gratitude as well as her hopes and requests.

I wondered if God had time to listen to her nightly outpourings, but supposed He would take good care of anyone who prayed as hard and long as she did.

We all went to the Japanese Union Church on Sundays, and Obah San was always the first one ready. Dressed in her best clothes, wearing her hat and gloves, she would sit on the sofa, patiently waiting for the rest of us to get ready.

She did the same thing if we invited her to go with us to see a movie. Obah San loved going out, and was always ready to have a good time with her grandchildren.

Because she'd never had much in life, she was always frugal and careful. She never let any food go to waste, and any fruit that was beginning to spoil had to be eaten before we could touch the good fruit. Sometimes if we were asked whether we'd like a banana or a peach, we would automatically respond, "Which one's spoiling?" and eat that one first.

Obah San had only a few clothes hanging in her closet, and toward the end of her life, she pinned a note on her best black dress that read, "This one is for my trip to Heaven."

When she had a big party at church on her eighty-eighth birthday, I asked her if she'd be able to blow out all the candles on her cake. "Don't worry," she said, smiling, and when the time came, she calmly took a fan from her purse and extinguished the candles with one grand gesture. I thought she was just great.

Not many of my Nisei friends had grandparents living in the United States, since most of them had remained behind in Japan. I was lucky to have at least one grandmother I could see once in a while, and in 1934 I was lucky enough to visit my other grandmother who lived in Japan.

9

FOREIGNER IN JAPAN

I was twelve when we sailed on the *Chichibu Maru* to visit my Grandmother Umegaki in Japan. My parents had taken me once before when I was two, but since I didn't remember that visit, I felt it didn't count. This time we were taking along our Los Angeles grandmother for her first visit to Japan since her departure so many years before.

I considered this my first ocean voyage, although I had gone often with my parents to see friends off at the drafty San Francisco piers. We would be among dozens of well-wishers crowding on board the ship to visit friends in state-rooms bursting with luggage, flowers, and baskets of fruit. Caught up in the festive excitement, I used to wish *I* were the one sailing off to Japan.

When one of the cabin boys traveled through the corridors beating the brass gong, however, I always felt a cold chill run down my spine.

"Come on, Papa," I would urge. "That's the 'all ashore that's going ashore' gong. Let's go."

But Papa continued talking with his friends, totally ignoring the urgent banging of the gong. By the time the passengers moved to the deck to throw rolls of colored tape to their friends below, the rest of us hurried down the narrow gangplank.

Papa, however, was still on board, smiling and waving from the upper deck. He would throw a roll of blue tape to my sister and a pink one to me.

"Come on, Papa!" we would shriek. "Hurry up!"

Finally, minutes before the gangplank was pulled up, he would saunter down, calmly saying, "Don't worry, they would never sail with me still on board."

Papa had a permanent dock pass to board the ships, and he came so often to meet friends or to see people off that he seemed to know everybody. For him the ships were familiar territory, but to me they were exotic, majestic, and slightly mysterious.

But this time, at last, I didn't have to worry about Papa getting caught on board a departing ship. This time we were passengers. *We* were the ones sailing to Japan. *We* were the ones everybody had come to see off. The baskets of fruits and flowers in the stateroom from Papa's business friends were for *us*. So were the gardenia corsages and the bouquets of flowers.

Now *I* was the one throwing rolls of tape down to our friends on the pier and waving and calling good-bye.

As the ship slowly eased out into San Francisco Bay, the wind tugged at the streamers I held in my hand. But I wouldn't let go. I hung on until the ship snatched them from the hands of the friends we'd left behind, and I watched as they fluttered off into the sky looking like a flying rainbow.

"Hey, we're really going!" I said to Keiko. "We're really going to Japan!"

But ten minutes after we had sailed through the Golden Gate, the ship began to pitch and roll, and my happy grin soon disappeared. The ever-present smell of bouillon I'd found so inviting earlier now made me turn green. All of us except Papa took to our bunks and stayed there for the next four days.

When we were finally able to join Papa in the dining salon, our waiters were so pleased to have a full table to serve, they broke into applause as we appeared.

By this time all shipboard activities were in full swing, and Keiko and I worked hard to catch up. We played shuffleboard and deck tennis. We had hot bouillon served by white-coated boys who rolled the soup cart up and down the decks each morning at ten o'clock. We went to every afternoon tea, stuffing ourselves with little cakes and fancy sandwiches, and amazingly had room for a big dinner in the evening.

One night there was a sukiyaki party on the lantern-festooned deck. For once I didn't have to set the table and neither Mama nor Papa had to cook. *We* were the company, and I was delighted that the ship's waiters did all the work. The Deans of Women of Mills College and the University of California in Berkeley happened to sit at our table, and we showed them how to use chopsticks and eat Japanese food.

"You'll have to send one of your daughters to each of us," they teased Mama and Papa. And that is exactly what happened. Keiko went to Mills College and I went to UC Berkeley.

The day a costume party was scheduled, Keiko and I

worked all day to prepare for it. She wore a pair of Papa's pants and suspenders, drew a mustache on her face, and squashed one of his hats on her head.

I dressed up like a doll, painting round circles of rouge on my cheeks. We tied strings to my wrists and ankles, attached them to two sticks, and went to the costume party as Tony the puppeteer and his doll puppet. We were beside ourselves when we won first prize.

By the time we neared Yokohama, I was so charmed with the good life on board the *Chichibu Maru,* I didn't want to get off.

Mama, on the other hand, could hardly wait. The morning we docked, she was up early. As our ship slid noiselessly alongside the pier, she impulsively pushed open one of the cabin's portholes to scan the faces on the pier.

Suddenly I heard her shout, "Oka San! Mother!"

It was a voice I had never heard before—filled with the longing and anguish of years of separation and a joy mingled with tears.

This was a Mama I'd never known before. For the first time in my life, I saw her not just as Mama who cooked and washed and sewed for us, but as someone's daughter. She was a person with a life and feelings of her own quite apart from mine.

For a fleeting moment I thought I understood the turmoil of her uprooted soul. But in the excitement of landing, the feeling passed, and she became once more the Mama I had always known.

None of us ever dreamed then of the terrible war that would separate her from her family and homeland forever.

It was a wonder to me how Mama could have left behind such a nice family and so many good friends. We met them all while we were in Japan.

Grandmother Umegaki was a plump, friendly woman

with a quiet manner that belied her strength. It was that hidden strength that gave her the courage to send her oldest daughter to America, and I believe my mother had a good measure of it in herself as well.

Mama's brother, Yukio, was a silversmith who made all sorts of beautiful gifts for us—a copper hanging engraved with my mother's favorite wildflower, a silver pin of my dog for me, and an engraved silver buckle for Keiko.

Another brother, Minoru, was a college professor who was writing several scholarly books and also painted quite well. I wasn't sure how to behave in front of Seizo, the brother who had become a priest, but he turned out to be the most fun of all and a skilled artist as well.

All three uncles wrote wonderful illustrated letters to my sister and me until the war ended their correspondence, and the life of one uncle as well.

Mama's only sister, Kiyo, was a widow who had lost a baby son and lived with her only daughter. They both seemed permanently saddened by their losses and had none of the easy laughter that dwelled in Mama and her brothers.

We were surrounded by family in Japan, since two of Papa's sisters had returned to live there as well. One lived in Osaka and the other in Tokyo. Wherever we went, we seemed to have a place to stay. Our relatives simply spread out some quilts for us on the *tatami* mat, enclosed us in great billowing mosquito netting, and we were set for the night.

One of the happiest times for my parents and Grandma Uchida was our stay in Kyoto, with its temples and hills and their beloved Doshisha University. The first friends Obah San wanted to visit were Dr. and Mrs. Learned, for whom she had worked so long ago.

They seemed so old and frail to me, like pale white

shadows in a sea of Japanese faces. They showered us with love and affection, and gave Keiko and me the American names we had long wanted to have. Keiko was named Grace, and I was given the name Ruth. But somehow it didn't make me as happy as I thought it would. I just didn't feel like a Ruth, and I never used the name.

Keiko and I tolerated innumerable long dinners and lunches with our parents' many friends, but when things got too boring, we would count the number of times people bowed to each other. In Japan no one hugged or shook hands. They just bowed. And bowed. And bowed some more. My mother set the record, with thirteen bows exchanged in one encounter.

What I liked best was going to temples and shrines on festival days, when the celebration, with costumed dancers and booming drums, was like a holiday parade and carnival rolled into one.

But I liked the celebration of Obon (All Souls' Day), too. That was when the spirits of the dead were believed to return home, and some families lit tiny bonfires at their front gate to welcome them at dusk. Inside, there were tables laden with all sorts of delicious dishes, prepared especially for the returning spirits.

In Japan the dead seemed to blend in with the living, as though there were no great black separation by death. And I found that a comforting thought.

Sometimes we climbed wooded hills that rose behind ancient temples to visit graveyards filled with moss-covered tombstones. And one day we went to pay our respects to our samurai grandfathers whom we had never known. Using small wooden scoops, we poured cold water on their tombstones to refresh their spirits, and left them handfuls of summer lilies.

I wondered what they thought of us—their grandchildren from far-off America, dressed in strange clothing and babbling in a foreign tongue. I hoped they liked us.

Once we stayed with an uncle and some cousins at a rural inn, where at the end of the day, we all went to the communal tub to have a pleasant soak together.

Then, wearing cool cotton kimonos provided by the inn, we gathered around the low table, where the maids brought us miso soup, broiled eel, and slivered cucumber on individual black lacquer trays.

After dinner we sat on the veranda and had sweet bean paste cakes and tea, watching a full moon rise over the mountains. The talk was gentle, and whenever it stopped, we could hear the swarms of cicadas in the pine trees buzzing in unison like some demented chorus.

As I sat watching the fireflies darting about in the darkness, I thought maybe I could get quite used to living in Japan. Here, at least, I looked like everyone else. Here, I blended in and wasn't always the one who was different.

And yet, I knew I was really a foreigner in Japan. I had felt like a complete idiot when an old woman asked me to read a bus sign for her, and I had to admit I couldn't read Japanese.

Deep down inside, where I really dwelled, I was thoroughly American. I missed my own language and the casual banter with friends. I longed for hot dogs and chocolate sodas and bathrooms with plumbing.

But the sad truth was, in America, too, I was perceived as a foreigner.

So what was I anyway, I wondered. I wasn't really totally American, and I wasn't totally Japanese. I was a mixture of the two, and I could never be anything else.

We often had formal family portraits taken when Grandmother Uchida visited us from Los Angeles.

My sister, Keiko, (right) and myself, when she was about seven and I was about three.

A page from my first diary — my farewell to Brownie.

My first brown wrapping paper book.

Having a good time with our neighbors. Left to right, Solveig, Yoshiko, Marian, Keiko.

My sister (waving), and I (bending), on a picnic with my Uncle Minoru and a cousin in Japan.

*With Kay on the day I received
my Masters in Education degree
from Smith College.*

*Our concentration camp in
Topaz, Utah. The barbed wire
fence and guard towers are
not visible.*

Laddie Loves Yoshi
Laddie Yoshi
Yoshi Loves Laddie

Feb. 19, 1933.
A dog at last! A stitch Collie too. We named him Laddie. He's tan with a big white neck. The boy that brought him said he had a pedigree. His yard is way in the back where it's nice and sunny. We're going to let him sleep in the house at night until he gets used to his yard outside. We are keeping him in his yard at day time. He's a darling dog.

Feb. 20, 1933
This morning we got up at 7:15 instead of around 7:30 on account of Laddie. (mama ought to be glad)

(Above) A page from "My Diary of Important Events."
(Below) My sister and I with Laddie on our back porch.

Oakland
July 1948

Our family in happier days after WW II.

Since we were not allowed to have cameras, I painted this scene of a dust storm in Topaz. (Watercolor).

Our family on the day Kay and I left Topaz.

10
UNHAPPY DAYS

I thought being at Edison Junior High School was going to be a great adventure, but I hadn't counted on the earthquake in Long Beach. It not only shook up Southern California, it awakened the school boards of Northern California to the dangers of its schools as well. It also shook up my entire life. I was in seventh grade at the time.

Edison was an old two-story redbrick building and one of the first schools in Berkeley to be condemned as unsafe. The whole school buzzed with rumors that it was closing, and one morning we finally learned the sad truth. Half the school would be sent to Burbank Junior High, and the other half, in which I was included, to Willard Junior High.

Willard was on Telegraph Avenue, about six blocks east of our house on Stuart Street, closer to the beautiful homes in the hills where affluent white families lived.

We knew several Japanese American college students who worked for board and room in these homes as "school boys" or "school girls," and frequently picked them up on our way to church. But that was about the only time I ventured into that area.

I was well aware of the unwritten law among the city's realtors that houses above certain streets would not be rented (and certainly not sold) to Asian families. I knew why no Japanese lived above Telegraph Avenue.

I was nervous and scared about going to Willard. With each block I walked toward the school, I became more and more insecure.

I think it was about then that I became reluctant to start a conversation with a white person, unless it was someone I knew well. I was perfectly at ease with our many good white friends, but more than anything, I dreaded being ignored by other people.

I knew what it was to feel unwanted in certain shops or restaurants or hotels. I knew how it felt to have a salesperson look through me as though I weren't there, waiting on a white person first. I couldn't bear the thought of being ignored by classmates I would see every day. So mostly I kept my mouth shut.

One day at assembly I sat next to a girl I knew slightly, but pretended not to notice her. It was only after she turned and asked, "Yoshi, aren't you going to talk to me?" that I could smile and become the friendly self I really wanted to be.

In spite of myself, however, I made some good white friends, and three are still my friends today. There was Sylvia, who invited me to join the Girl Reserves and took me under her wing. I loved being part of that group and never missed a meeting. I went to several annual Girl Reserves conferences and had my first camp experience at their summer camp in the Sierras.

Once when our group was to be photographed for the local newspaper, however, the photographer casually tried to ease me out of the picture. I knew why, and so did Sylvia.

"Come on, Yoshi," she said, grabbing my arm. "Stand next to me."

We linked arms and stood firm.

"Smile," the photographer said with a dour look.

And standing together in our white middies and skirts and our blue Girl Reserves ties, Sylvia and I smiled.

Another friend was red-haired Libby, who lived in one of the beautiful hill homes I could only dream about. Yet she didn't seem to mind at all that I lived in the flatlands. She whispered to me in French class and giggled with me in gym and treated me no differently from her white friends.

There was also Bob, a popular curly-haired blond with an infectious grin, who sat across the aisle from me in my homeroom. He always had a friendly word for me then and still does.

It always came as something of a surprise whenever a white student was nice to me. If I hadn't been so fearful of opening myself up to my classmates, there probably would have been others who might have befriended me.

Unfortunately, society had caused me to have so little self-esteem and to feel so inferior, I was careful to close myself up to insure against being hurt.

There were few teachers at Willard that I cared for. I had an intense dislike for Mrs. C., my English teacher, who never let anyone explain anything.

"I was sick," a student might begin, trying to tell her why his or her homework wasn't finished. But Mrs. C. would always interrupt, saying, "The hot place is paved with excuses." And that was the end of the conversation.

I don't know what Mrs. C. thought of my argument in a class debate over whether the Bay Bridge should be built. I loved the ferries and argued that the bridge should not be built.

Fortunately, nobody listened to me, and the bridge was opened on November 11, 1936. We crossed the span for the first time on the fourteenth, and I sincerely hoped Mrs. C. had forgotten my earlier error in judgment. I certainly didn't want to go to the "hot place" for that.

Another teacher I disliked was my ancient-history teacher. She wore the same brown crepe dress day after day, until I could see the grime gathering at the neckline. I wonder what she would think if she knew that I have forgotten every date she made me memorize, but can picture so clearly that ugly brown dress.

High school was even worse. Like most of the students at Willard, I enrolled in University High School in Oakland instead of going to Berkeley High. Uni, as we called it, was on the cutting edge of the progressive education movement, and my sister (by now we called her Kay) had gone there, too.

My friends Sylvia and Libby were also at Uni, and I made other friends as well. I went to football games with my new friends and even visited some of their homes. But gradually I sensed the lives of my white classmates moving in new directions, involving parties and boys, in which I had no part. Even if I had been invited, however, I would not have gone.

To add to my general discontent, most of my classes were uninspired and boring. After all, how much can you learn in a class called "Personal Management"? Overall I got good grades, but I was terrible in gym. I could barely hit a volleyball over the net, and I always struck out when we played softball. It was humiliating.

I could hardly wait to get out. I studied hard, took extra classes, and graduated from high school in two and a half years so I could enter the university in the fall.

I was sixteen when I became a freshman at the University of California in Berkeley. At the time, Japanese Americans were excluded from the white world of sororities and fraternities, but we did have an alternative.

I found a new Nisei community in the Japanese Men's and Women's Student Clubs, where I felt comfortable and accepted. I plunged quickly into all their social activities, and here at last, late bloomer that I was, I finally discovered the pleasures of dating.

11
GLORY
DAYS

Even before I was writing my short stories in the sixth grade, I used to pretend I was a teacher. I would sit at my desk, take the roll of an imaginary class, and teach my silent pupils how to spell or make neat Os in penmanship.

I thought I could be a good teacher. But I knew that few, if any, Japanese Americans or other minorities were being hired by the public schools. It was just a dream, I thought, that could never come true.

So when I entered the university, I didn't even consider education as a possible major. Instead, I majored in English, philosophy, and history, without a clue as to how I would earn a living when I graduated. I supposed I could always get a job as a secretary since I had learned how to type.

I didn't study very hard at Cal (as everyone called the

University) and not much was required of me. The world then was a simpler place. Most of the students were naive and immature, and we didn't concern ourselves about much beyond our campus community.

I went with my Nisei friends to every home football game, and a group of us even followed our team to Los Angeles for a crucial game with UCLA. The merriment began on the train jammed with noisy, boisterous students and continued through the entire weekend. I don't even recall who won, but it really didn't matter. We just celebrated anyway.

My days of pre-trip fevers were long gone, and now that I had finally caught up with my cousins (and even my sister), we all enjoyed socializing together. On one visit, when we went dancing to a big-name band at the Palladium, we saw Barbara Stanwyck. And we often went to the glittering Grauman's Chinese Theatre for stargazing as well as movie viewing. When a friend took me dancing at the Coconut Grove one night, I thought life couldn't get much better.

It was an exciting and glorious time. My diary was filled with accounts of open houses, weiner roasts, visits to the Exposition on Treasure Island, or descriptions of the Spring Hop, the Fall Informal, the Senior Fling, and all the other dances that crowded our college calendar.

In this world where I was totally accepted, I no longer felt the need to close myself up. I became president of the Japanese Women's Student Club one year. I was also active in an annual Northern California Conference for Nisei Christians, sometimes chairing committees or discussion groups.

I wasn't totally separated from the white world, however, for our family had several close white friends who came for dinner or invited us to their homes. The president of the Pacific School of Religion (my earlier nemesis) often came with his wife and football-player son for sukiyaki dinners.

As Papa cooked one pan of sukiyaki after another, he would ask the husky young man if he cared for more.

"Just a little more," he would answer, holding out his plate. He often had eight or nine helpings, and I refilled his rice bowl just as many times.

As I scraped up the last of the rice, I used to worry that we would run out of food. "Leave room for dessert," I would say. But I needn't have worried, he always had room for at least two slices of Mama's whipped-cream banana cake.

Mama spent hours preparing her dinners, for she considered her meals a gift from the heart. For our birthdays or any other special events in our lives, Mama always made our favorite Japanese dish, which was an extra gift in addition to whatever else we were given. Everything she made tasted so good, it was no wonder everyone liked coming to our house for dinner.

By the time I was in college, however, our company dinners sometimes caused me much embarrassment. This was because our only telephone was on a desk by the window in the dining room.

When I began dating, the one thing I dreaded most was getting a phone call in the middle of one of our dinner parties. And, of course, one night it happened.

A friend called to invite me to the Spring Hop. The minute I said, "Hi, Joe," the conversation at the table came to a stop. Everyone was more interested in hearing what I said than in the conversation at the table.

I turned my back and hid behind the drapes, hoping that might muffle my voice.

"What color is your dress, Yo?" Joe asked thoughtfully. He would send a corsage that matched.

"Uh, pink, I guess. No, wait, maybe blue. Uh . . . I don't know . . . I'm not sure yet . . ." All I could think about was that everyone was listening to me.

Ending the conversation as quickly as possible, I emerged red-faced from my drapery cocoon. Everyone was grinning and giving me knowing looks, as though each had uncovered all my deepest secrets. I was absolutely mortified.

During another lively dinner party, my father answered the phone. "It's for you, Yo," he said. "It's a young man."

But when I got to the phone, no one was there. Whoever called had probably heard all the laughter and gotten cold feet. I never did find out who it was and nearly perished from curiosity.

My father was also a problem in other ways. Both he and my mother enjoyed young people and always came to meet our dates before we went out. I didn't mind that, but Papa, friendly soul that he was, usually wanted to have a nice, long conversation with them.

"Where are you from?" he would begin.

The answer could be Fresno, or Stockton, or Los Angeles, or Guadalupe. My father knew people everywhere because of his many contacts in the Federation of Japanese Churches. He would keep us fidgeting while he carried on a lively conversation, asking about everyone he knew in my friend's hometown.

Then Papa would say, "Why don't you young people start your dances earlier? If you started at seven o'clock instead of nine o'clock, you'd all get home earlier. Wouldn't that make more sense?"

At this point I would finally say, "Oh, Papa, for heaven's sake!" and steer my friend out the door. Papa couldn't understand why we started out so late and never failed to ask us as we left the house.

My sister had her own embarrassing moments. The worst happened one rainy night. She had just said good night to her date, when he slipped on our slippery front steps and slid ingloriously on his bottom all the way to the pavement.

My mother, never one to ignore a problem, especially if

it caused anyone distress, took quick action. She applied black adhesive tape on each step for better traction. Then using white paint, she printed the message "Please watch your step"—one word to a step.

The trouble was, she began at the bottom and worked her way up. So when friends left the house, they read the puzzling message "Step your watch please." But no one slipped after that, and everyone left our house laughing.

All during my college years and for many years after, I dated only Nisei men, never going out socially with a white man. But eventually the world changed, and I changed, too. Then a man who happened to be white became my special friend and remained so for over twenty years.

It was during my senior year at Cal, as I looked forward to graduating in five months, that my happy, carefree life came to an abrupt end. It was December 1941. And one sunny Sunday morning, Japan bombed Pearl Harbor.

12
BECOMING A "NONALIEN"

"No company for lunch?" I asked, surprised.

It was Sunday, but there were only the four of us going home from church. It seemed strange, but I was glad for the peace and quiet. Finals were starting soon at the university, and I was anxious to have a quick lunch and go to the library to study.

As we were having lunch, an urgent voice suddenly broke into the program on the radio. Japan, the announcer said, had attacked Pearl Harbor.

"Oh, no!" Mama gasped. "It must be a mistake."

"Of course it is," Papa agreed.

He turned up the volume. It didn't sound like a mistake.

"It's probably the work of some fanatic," Papa insisted.

Not one of us believed it was war. Kay went with my

parents to visit friends, and I went to the campus library to study. I didn't return until almost five o'clock.

The minute I got home, I knew something was wrong. A strange man sat in our living room, and my father was gone.

Mama and Kay explained that two FBI men had taken my father for questioning. A third remained to guard us, intercepting all phone calls and preventing friends from coming to see us.

"We're prisoners in our own home," Kay said ominously. "The police even broke in and searched our house while we were out."

As upset as she was, in her usual thoughtful way, Mama was making tea for the FBI man in the kitchen. She always served tea to anyone who called, even the "Real Silk Lady," who came with her satchel of silken samples to sell Mama stockings and undergarments.

"You're making tea for the FBI man?" I asked, indignant.

But Mama respected everybody regardless of the work they did. The man who delivered our dry cleaning, the People's Bread man who sold doughnuts and bread from his truck, the boy who delivered rice and tofu from the Japanese grocery store, or the Watkins door-to-door salesman. She treated them all with equal respect and courtesy.

"He's only doing his job," Mama said now of the FBI man. "He's trying to be pleasant." And she carried a tray of tea things into the living room.

But I wasn't about to have tea with someone guarding us as though we were prisoners. I went to my bedroom and stayed there until the FBI man got instructions to leave.

When at last the three of us were alone, we made supper, but none of us felt like eating. Papa was gone, and we had no idea what happened to him or when he would be back. We finally went to bed, leaving the porch light on for him.

As I lay in bed in my cold, dark room, I heard the mournful wail of the foghorns on the bay. I felt a clammy fear come over me, as though I was at the bottom of a deep well and couldn't climb out.

My father didn't return that night or for the next three days. We had no idea where he was or what had happened to him. But Mama persuaded me to continue going to classes, and somehow I managed to get through my finals.

Five days after he was taken, we finally learned that my father was being held at the Immigration Detention Quarters in San Francisco with about one hundred other Japanese men.

The FBI had apprehended all the leaders of the Japanese American community—businessmen, teachers, bankers, farmers, fishermen—and held them incommunicado.

The following day we got a postcard from Papa asking us to send his shaving kit and some clean clothing. We arranged for permission to visit him, and Kay drove us to San Francisco.

My heart sank when I saw the drab gray building that looked like a jail. And as though to confirm my impression, a guard brought Papa to the visiting room like a prisoner.

"Papa! Are you all right?"

He looked tired and haggard, but assured us that he was fine. The news he gave us, however, was terrible. All the men in his group were being sent in a few days to a prisoner-of-war camp in Missoula, Montana.

"Montana! Then we won't be able to visit you anymore."

"I know," Papa answered, "but we can write to each other. Now, girls, be strong, and take good care of Mama for me, will you?"

Kay and I began to cry as we said our good-byes and watched Papa go back down the bleak hallway. It was Mama who was the strong one.

From the moment we were at war with Japan, my parents (and all the Issei) had suddenly become "enemy aliens." They were not citizens because by law the United States prevented Asians from becoming naturalized citizens. Now Kay, as the oldest U.S. citizen, became head of our household.

She had graduated from Mills College in 1940 with a degree in early childhood education, but the only job she could find was as a nursemaid to a three-year-old white child. Her employers asked her to stay on in spite of the war, but I wondered why they felt compelled to say that. After all, Kay was still the same person, and she was an American, just as they were.

However, strange ideas seemed to be erupting in the minds of many Americans. I was astonished when a white friend of many years asked, "Didn't you have any idea it was going to happen?"

I was hurt that she had asked. Her question implied that we somehow knew of Japan's war plans simply because we were Americans of Japanese ancestry. It was a ridiculous assumption.

Eventually Kay left her job to devote all her time to managing our household affairs. Papa's bank account had been blocked immediately, and for a while we could withdraw only $100 a month for living expenses. She needed important papers from his safe-deposit box, but found that the FBI had confiscated all his keys.

She needed to pay the premiums on his car and life insurance policies, file his income tax returns, and at his request, purchase U.S. Defense Bonds. It was a difficult job for Kay, trying to manage all the tasks that Papa had handled until then.

Papa wrote often, trying to help us manage without him, but his letters often arrived looking like lace doilies. The censors had cut out whatever they didn't want us to read.

"Don't forget to lubricate the car," Papa wrote. Or, "Be sure to have the roses pruned, brush Laddie every day, send Grandma her monthly check, and take our Christmas offering to church."

We could tell he was trying to anticipate all our problems from his snowbound camp in Montana. He also tried to cheer us up, and asked us to tell our church friends not to be too discouraged.

Still, it was hard not to worry. Japan was now the despised enemy, and every Japanese American became a target of the same hatred directed at Japan. It was not because we had done anything wrong, but simply because we *looked* like the enemy.

Once again, my Japanese face was going to cause me misery.

One evening I went out with some friends for a late evening snack to a restaurant where we'd often gone before. We hadn't been there long when an angry Filipino man came to our table. His fists were clenched, and his eyes flashed with anger.

"You know what your Jap soldiers are doing to my homeland?" he shouted. "They're killing my people!"

"But we're not from Japan," we said, trying to reason with him. "We're Americans!"

He continued to harass us, not listening to anything we said. Then having had his say, he left, still scowling. But he had ruined our evening, for we knew there were many others who hated us as much as he did. We left the restaurant quickly and went home in silence.

I was frightened as I saw newspaper accounts accusing Japanese Americans of spying and sabotage in Hawaii. These rumors were later completely refuted, but at the time most Americans accepted them as the truth.

THE INVISIBLE THREAD

Soon racist groups began calling for a forced eviction of all Americans of Japanese ancestry along the West Coast. They called it an "evacuation"—a word implying removal for the protection of the person being removed—but actually it was an uprooting.

Hatred against Asians, however, was not new to California. It had existed for a hundred years. Laws that restricted immigration and land ownership already existed, and now groups who would benefit economically from our removal joined in the calls for a mass uprooting.

As new rumors spread, we grew more and more uneasy. Several of my classmates from out of town left the university to rejoin their families. And in Montana my father worried helplessly about what would happen to us.

We thought we should start packing some of our belongings, in case we were actually uprooted. One evening, as we were packing books into wooden crates, a friend stopped by to see us.

"What on earth are you doing?" he asked. "There will never be a mass evacuation. Don't you realize we're American citizens? The U.S. government would never intern its own citizens. It would be unconstitutional."

Of course his facts were right. Still, we knew that the attorney general of California claimed, incorrectly, that Japanese Americans had "infiltrated . . . every strategic spot" in the state.

On the floor of the House of Representatives, Congressman John Rankin had shouted, "I say it is of vital importance that we get rid of every Japanese . . . Damn them! Let us get rid of them now!"

Our government did nothing to stop these hysterical outcries or to refute the false rumors. We learned many years later that although President Franklin D. Roosevelt had seen a state department report testifying to the "extraordinary degree of loyalty" among the West Coast Japanese

68

Americans, he chose instead to listen to the voices of the hatemongers.

On February 19, 1942, the President signed Executive Order 9066, which resulted in the forcible eviction of all Japanese, "aliens and nonaliens," from the West Coast of the United States. He stated that this was a military necessity, and because we did not know otherwise at the time, we believed him. The Supreme Court of the land sanctioned his decision.

It was a sad day for all Americans of Japanese ancestry. Our government no longer considered us its citizens, simply referring to us as "nonaliens." It also chose to ignore the Fifth and Fourteenth Amendments to the Constitution that guaranteed "due process of law" and "equal protection under the law for all citizens." We were to be imprisoned in concentration camps without a trial or hearing of any kind.

"But we're at war with Germany and Italy, too," I objected. "Why are only the Japanese Americans being imprisoned?"

No one, including our government, had an answer for that.

Under the direction of Lieutenant General John L. DeWitt of the Western Defense Command, 120,000 men, women, and children of Japanese ancestry (two-thirds of whom were American citizens), were to be uprooted from their homes on the West Coast of the United States.

We were told we could "evacuate voluntarily" outside the military zone, but most of us had no place to go. How could we suddenly pick up everything and move to a new and unknown location? Some of our friends moved to inland towns, but when the exclusion zone was later extended, they were uprooted once again and eventually interned in a camp anyway.

We felt like prisoners even before our actual eviction. We had to observe an 8:00 P.M. curfew and were not permitted to travel more than five miles beyond our home. We had to turn in all shortwave radios, cameras, binoculars, and fire-arms. We also had to register. Each family was given a number, and ours was 13453.

I shuddered when I read the headlines of our local paper on April 21. It read, "JAPS GIVEN EVACUATION ORDERS HERE." On May 1, we were to be sent to the Tanforan Racetrack, which had been hurriedly converted into an "Assembly Center."

"But how can we clear out our house in only ten days?" Mama asked desperately. "We've lived here for fifteen years!"

"I guess we just have to do it, Mama," Kay answered. "We can't argue with the U.S. Army."

Friends came to help us clear out our belongings. But no one could help us decide what to keep and what to discard. We had to do that for ourselves. We grew frantic as the days went by. We sold furniture we should have kept and stored things we should have thrown out.

Mama was such a saver. She had drawers and closets and cartons overflowing with memory-laden belongings. She saved everything from old string and wrapping paper to valentines, Christmas cards, clay paperweights, and draw-ings that Kay and I had made for her. She had dozens of photograph albums and guest books and packets of old let-ters from friends and family.

"How can I throw all this away?" she asked bleakly.

In the end she just put everything in trunks that we stored at the Bekins Storage Company. We also stored there the furniture that was too large to be left with friends offering us space in their basements.

We put off until the last minute a decision none of us wanted to make. What were we going to do with our be-loved Laddie? We knew no friends who could take him.

Finally, it occurred to me to put an ad in the *Daily Californian* at the university.

"I am one of the Japanese American students soon to be evacuated," I wrote, "and have a male Scotch collie that can't come with me. Can anyone give him a home? If interested, please call me immediately at Berkeley 7646W."

The day my ad appeared, I was deluged with sympathetic calls, but we gave him to the first boy who called because he seemed kind and caring. We gave him Laddie's doghouse, leash, brushes, favorite toy, and everything else he would need.

The boy promised he would write us at Tanforan to let us know how Laddie was doing. We each gave Laddie a hug and watched him climb reluctantly into the strange car.

"Be a good boy now, Laddie," I said. "We'll come back for you someday."

Mama, Kay, and I couldn't bear to go inside. We stood at the curb watching as the boy drove off. And we could still hear Laddie's plaintive barking even after the car turned the corner and we could no longer see it.

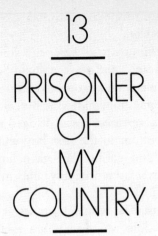

13
PRISONER
OF
MY
COUNTRY

Papa's beautiful garden was now full of gaping holes.
Mama had dug up a few favorite plants to give to her
friends, and the others were given to people like the woman
who stopped by one day to ask if she could have some gladiolas. "Since you're leaving anyway . . ." she said, smiling
awkwardly.

Our rented house was now a barren shell, with only three
mattresses left on the floor. In the corner of Mama's room
was a large shapeless canvas blanket bag that we called our
Camp Bundle. We tossed into it all the things we were instructed to take with us—sheets, blankets, pillows, dishes,
and eating utensils. We also added our own list of necessi-
ties—boots, umbrellas, flashlights, teacups, a hot plate, a
kettle, and anything else we thought might be useful in
camp.

"You know, we're supposed to bring only what we can carry," Kay warned.

We practiced lifting our suitcases and found that we could each carry two. But what were we to do about the Camp Bundle? Each day it grew and bulged like some living thing, and we had no idea how we would ever get it to camp.

Still, there was nothing we could do but continue to fill it, and to hope that somehow things would work out.

The night before we left, our Swiss neighbors invited us to dinner. Mrs. Harpainter made a delicious chicken dinner, served on her finest china and linens, reminding me of all the company dinners we'd had in our own house in happier days.

When we got home, Marian and Solveig came from next door to say good-bye, bringing gifts for each of us.

They hugged us, saying, "Come back soon!"

"We will," we answered. But we had no idea when or if we would ever come back.

The next morning Mrs. Harpainter brought us breakfast on a tray full of bright colorful dishes. She then drove us to the First Congregational Church of Berkeley, designated as the Civil Control Station where we were to report.

We said our good-byes quickly, unable to speak many words. Already the church grounds teemed with hundreds of bewildered Japanese Americans, clutching bundles tagged with their names and family number. Parked at the curb were rows of trucks being loaded with the larger baggage that could not be hand-carried.

"I wish they had told us there'd be trucks," Kay muttered. "We could have been spared all that worry about our Camp Bundle."

But the army didn't seem to care whether we worried or not. To them we were simply prisoners. They had stationed armed guards all around the church, their bayonets mounted and ready. It was only when I saw them that the full horror of the day struck me. My knees felt weak, and I almost lost my breakfast.

The First Congregational Church had been good to us. Many of its families had offered to store belongings for the departing Japanese Americans, and now the church women were serving tea and sandwiches. But none of us could eat.

We were soon loaded onto waiting buses and began our one-way journey down familiar streets, across the Bay Bridge, and down the Bayshore Highway. Although some people wept quietly, most of us were silent. We kept our eyes on the window, watching as familiar landmarks slipped away behind us one by one.

And then we were there—at the Tanforan Racetrack Assembly Center, one of fifteen such centers created at racetracks and fairgrounds along the West Coast to intern the Japanese Americans.

From the bus window I could see a high barbed-wire fence that surrounded the entire area, and at each corner of the camp was a guard tower manned by soldiers.

The gates swung open to receive the buses, and armed guards closed them behind us. We were now locked in and under twenty-four-hour guard.

We had always been law-abiding citizens. We had done nothing wrong. And yet, we had now become prisoners of our own country.

There was an enormous crowd gathered around the grandstand. One would have thought the horses were running, except that all the people there were Japanese of all ages, sizes, and shapes.

We scanned the crowd for familiar faces and were relieved to find several friends who had arrived a few days earlier from Oakland.

"Hey, Kay and Yo! Over here!"

They steered us through the crowds to an area where doctors peered down our throats and pronounced us healthy. Then they helped us find our way to Barrack 16, Apartment 40, to which we had been assigned.

"We get apartments?" I asked.

"Not the kind you're thinking of, Yo. Wait, you'll see." My friend knew I was in for a rude awakening.

Mama was wearing her hat, gloves, and Sunday clothes, simply because she never would have thought of leaving home any other way. In her good Sunday shoes, she was carefully picking her way over the puddles left in the muddy track by rain the day before.

The army had hastily constructed dozens of tar-papered barracks around the track and in the infield to house the eight thousand "evacuees," as we were called. Each barrack was divided into six rooms, one family to a room. But our barrack was not one of these.

Barrack 16 turned out to be nothing more than an old stable, with twenty-five stalls facing north, back to back with the same number facing south. Our so-called apartment was a small, dark horse stall, ten feet by twenty feet. I couldn't believe what I saw.

Dust, dirt, and wood shavings littered the linoleum, and I could still smell the manure that lay beneath it. There were two tiny windows on either side of the door (our only source of daylight), and the stall was divided into two sections by a Dutch door worn with teeth marks.

On the walls I saw tiny corpses of spiders and bugs that had been permanently whitewashed to the boards by the army painters. A single light bulb dangled from the ceiling, and three folded army cots lay on the dirty floor. This was to be our "home" for the next five months.

One of our friends found a broom and swept out our

stall, while two of the boys went to pick up our mattresses. Actually, they'd had to stuff the tickings with straw themselves.

Another friend loaned us some dishes and silverware since our big bundle hadn't yet been delivered. "We'd better leave soon for the mess hall before the lines for supper get too long," she warned.

Until smaller mess halls could be built throughout the camp, all meals were being served in the basement of the grandstand. Clutching our plates and silverware, we made our way back down the muddy track.

When we arrived at the grandstand, there were already several long weaving lines of people waiting to get in, and we were soon separated from our friends. Mama, Kay, and I took our places at the end of one line and huddled together to keep warm. A cold, piercing wind had begun to blow as the sun went down, and it scattered dust and debris in our faces.

I felt like a refugee standing in a soup line in some alien and forbidding land. It was not only degrading and humiliating, it seemed totally unreal—like some horrible nightmare.

Since we had missed lunch, I was eager for a nice hot meal, but supper consisted of a piece of butterless bread, two canned sausages, and a plain boiled potato. Everything was dropped onto our plates by two cooks, who picked up the food with their fingers from large dishpans.

We ate at picnic tables in the cold, damp basement crowded with hundreds of people, and even though I was still hungry, I couldn't wait to get back to our stall.

It was dark now, and the north wind was blowing into our stall from all the cracks around the windows and the door. We bundled up in our coats and sat on our prickly mattresses, too miserable even to talk.

Kay and I worried that the cold air would aggravate Mama's neuralgia, which caused terrible pain in her facial nerves.

"Are you OK, Mom?" we asked.

But Mama wasn't thinking about herself. "I wonder how Papa San is?" she said softly.

Then we heard a truck outside, and a voice called, "Hey Uchida! Apartment 40!"

As Kay and I rushed to the door calling, "That's us!" we saw two baggage boys wrestling our big Camp Bundle off their truck.

"What ya got in here anyways?" they asked good-naturedly. "Didja bring everything in your whole damn house?"

I was embarrassed. Our bundle was clearly the biggest and bulkiest object in their truck.

"It's just our pet rhinoceros," I quipped. And while the boys were still laughing, we dragged our monstrous bundle into the stall and quickly untied all the knots we'd labored over just that morning.

Everything we had tossed into its obliging depths now tumbled out looking like old friends.

"I'll go get some water," I volunteered.

I grabbed the kettle and hurried to the women's latrine-washroom about fifty yards from our stable. Kay and Mama, in the meantime, retrieved our sheets and blankets to make up the cots.

I had news for them when I returned.

"There're no doors to the toilets or showers," I reported, horrified. "And we have to wash up at long tin sinks that look like feeding troughs."

I had also taken a look at the laundry barrack with its rows of washtubs, where everything, including sheets and towels, were to be washed by hand. They were still empty, but by morning there would be long lines of people waiting to use the tubs.

Mama diverted our attention to matters at hand. "Well, we can at least make some tea now," she said.

We plugged the hot plate into a double socket we'd had the good sense to bring and waited for the water to boil.

Then came the first of many knocks we'd be hearing at our door, as friends discovered where we lived.

"Hey, Kay and Yo. Are you home?"

Four of my college friends had come by to see how we were doing, bringing along the only snack they could find—a box of dried prunes. Even the day before, I wouldn't have given the prunes a second look. But now they were as welcome as a box of the Maskey's chocolates Papa used to bring home from San Francisco.

We gathered around the warmth of the hot plate, sipping the tea Mama made for us, wondering how we had gotten ourselves into such an intolerable situation.

We were angry that our country had so cruelly deprived us of our civil rights. But we had been raised to respect and trust those in authority. Resistance or confrontation such as we know them today was unthinkable, for the world then was a totally different place.

There had yet been no freedom marches or demonstrations of protest. No one had yet heard of Martin Luther King, Jr. No one knew about ethnic pride. Most Americans were not concerned about civil rights and would not have supported us had we tried to resist the uprooting.

We naively believed at the time that cooperating with the government was the only way to prove our loyalty and to help our country. We did not know then, as we do today, how badly our leaders betrayed us and our country's democratic ideals.

They had imprisoned us with full knowledge that their action was not only unconstitutional, but totally unnecessary. They knew there was no military necessity for the mass uprooting, although that was the reason given for incarcerating us.

How could America—our own country—have done this to us? we wondered. And trying to cheer ourselves up, we talked about steaks and hamburgers and hot dogs as we munched on the cold dried prunes.

14

PRISON CAMP TEACHER

Someone was snoring in my ear. Annoyed to be awakened so early, I reached out to poke Kay. But instead, I felt my hand hit the rough partition that separated our stall from the neighbors. And suddenly I remembered where I was.

It wasn't Kay snoring at all. It was Eichi, the teenaged boy next door, who apparently slept just a few inches away from me on the other side of the partition.

It wasn't only the snoring. I could hear just about everything that went on in the neighboring stalls, including most conversations. The foot-high open space between the sloping stable roof and the partition tops made privacy something we could only dream about.

I often heard Eichi being scolded by his parents for going

80

off all day with his friends, returning late at night, and banging on the door to be let in.

"What's wrong with you, Eichi?" his mother would say. "Don't you know you wake up all the neighbors?"

But one Sunday it was his parents who had to do the banging. They had gone to one of the church services organized in camp and come home to find that they couldn't get in. Eichi was asleep in the rear of the stall with the door bolted from inside.

"Eichi! Wake up! Let us in!" his parents shouted.

But I could hear him snoring like a bear in hibernation.

"I'll wake him up," I offered, and grabbing our broom, I stood on my cot and lowered it over the partition. I poked and prodded, aiming for his face.

"Hey, Eichi!" I called. "Wake up!"

"Go 'way," Eichi grumbled.

It took a little more prodding, but Eichi finally opened the door with a foolish grin on his face. And as the curious onlookers cheered, his parents apologized profusely for the commotion they had caused. We all became good friends after that.

Our neighbors to the right weren't as appealing. They gambled and played cards all day and rarely spoke to us. Except for the day the woman found an empty barrel and rolled it back to her stall.

"It will make a fine bathtub, don't you think?" she asked.

The Issei weren't used to taking showers, and the highest compliment our neighbor could give anyone was to offer the use of her barrel for a nice warm soak.

On May 8, not only our two neighbors, but everyone up and down the length of our stable heard the jubilation in our stall. My father was unexpectedly released from Montana.

We knew many of our white friends had sent affidavits

81

and letters supporting his early release, but it wasn't until a wire from Papa arrived that we realized he would be home soon.

The next afternoon a messenger came to tell us that my father had arrived and was waiting for us in the administration building. Kay and I couldn't wait for Mama and ran ahead, racing down the track to the grandstand visitors' room. And there was Papa waiting for us. He looked tired and thinner, but otherwise he seemed all right.

"Papa!" we screamed. "Papa!"

He held out his arms and gathered us in. "I'm home, Kay and Yo," he said. "I'm home at last!"

News of my father's return spread quickly to all our friends scattered throughout the camp. Our church friends, Kay's friends, my friends, everyone we knew, came to our tiny stall to share our joy.

Papa had endless stories to tell about the prisoner-of-war camp in Montana where he and the other men were treated as "dangerous enemy aliens." He told how they had been stripped of all their possessions as they rode the heavily guarded train to Missoula, with the blinds lowered at all times.

All their incoming and outgoing mail was censored, and every scrap of paper removed from all packages. Canned goods were given to them with the labels removed, and boxes of chocolates were emptied out on the counter, forcing the men to scoop them up in their caps.

Papa was a lively conversationalist, and the neighboring stalls quieted down as everyone listened to him. But at 10:00 P.M. Mama reminded him that the neighbors needed their sleep, and our friends left quickly, knowing they could come again the next day to hear more.

We now had four cots crowded into our tiny stall, but at least we were all together, and that made life seem a little better.

What we needed in Tanforan was an instant community. The first thing required was a hospital, for there were people getting sick and having babies, and some were dying. We needed churches and recreation centers to provide people with constructive activities to fill the long empty hours of each day. And what the children needed most were schools.

Fortunately, there were many professionals among the internees who quickly organized and staffed these vital functions. Kay, along with a classmate from Mills College, organized the camp's first nursery schools and was able, at last, to make use of her training.

Recruited to help on her staff, I helped Kay prepare for the opening of her two nursery schools. I soon discovered, however, that working with three and four year olds was no easy task.

One day, when I took a few children for a walk, two of them ran home and refused to come back to school. On other days children screamed and cried, while others wet their pants and had to be cleaned up. Very soon I realized that I simply wasn't cut out to be a nursery-school teacher.

As soon as a call went out for elementary-school teachers, I applied for a job. There were four credentialed teachers in camp, and I was lucky to be assigned as assistant to one of them. She generously shared her expert knowledge and skills with me, and in the elementary schools, I finally felt at home.

After only a week, however, I was reassigned because of a shortage of teachers and suddenly found myself in full charge of a class of second graders. With no paper or pencils, books or crayons, I wondered what I would do for three hours with a roomful of restless children.

What I didn't realize was how much the children wanted to be in school. They were longing for a normal routine and needed school to give them the sense of security and order that had been snatched from them so abruptly.

Classes met wherever there was room. The high school students met under the grandstand by the parimutuel windows. My class met in a barrack used on Sundays by the Buddhist church, but was canceled the first day because the building was needed for a funeral.

I discovered I could actually keep a class of second graders interested in what I said. This wasn't play-pretend any more. I was a bona fide teacher, even if only in a makeshift camp school, and I loved being with the children. Discovering where I lived, a covey of them would escort me to and from school every day. I couldn't hide from them even if I'd wanted to.

Eventually books and supplies trickled in from the outside. We also had daily teachers' meetings, not only to make lesson plans, but to put in our time for a forty-four-hour work week. Our salary was $16 a month, and my first paycheck, with deductions for sick days, was exactly $6.38.

Our schools held open houses, organized a PTA, and participated in campwide programs such as the Flag Day ceremony. The children of my class, many of them dressed in their best clothes, sang "America, the Beautiful" for the occasion. They also recited the Pledge of Allegiance to the flag, unaware of the irony of the words they spoke. We all honored the flag of our country, just as we always had.

I often felt so inadequate as a teacher, but felt a little better when I finally received my diploma from the university, making my BA degree official.

It arrived one day in a cardboard roll and was handed to me in my horse stall by the mailman. I was pleased to see that I had graduated with honors. I had missed wearing a cap and gown and attending my commencement by only two weeks, and read about the ceremony in the local newspaper.

I saw that a Nisei classmate had won the University Medal for highest scholastic achievement in our graduating class. The president explained that the winner of the medal was unable to attend the ceremonies because "his country had called him elsewhere."

Being healthy in camp was bad enough, but being sick was total misery. Kay and I both caught terrible colds and spent several dreary days in the "dungeon"—the dark, windowless rear half of our stall.

One afternoon I heard Mama answer a knock on our door and a small voice ask, "Is Miss Uchida home?"

"Yes, she is," Mama answered. "She's in bed with a bad cold."

I recognized little Keizo's voice, put on my robe, and went out to see him.

"How was class today?" I asked.

He grinned proudly and gave me a large sheet of paper on which he had written the word *boy* about thirty times.

"See," he explained. "Every time a boy was bad, I wrote down *boy*.

"Oh, I see. Thank you. Did the teacher have a hard time?"

Keizo nodded. "I'll say. You better come back quick."

I went back to school the next day, just as much for myself as for the poor substitute. I couldn't stand the thought of spending one more dreary day in the "dungeon."

Kay, however, wasn't as lucky. She couldn't shake off a temperature that lingered for almost a month.

"You'll never get well if you keep getting out of bed," Mama warned. "We'll carry all your meals back to you from now on."

"But I'll still have to go to the latrine," Kay argued.

Papa solved that problem by finding a large tin can for her at the mess hall. But Kay was still worried.

"I don't want the whole stable to hear me every time I have to go," she pointed out.

I certainly didn't blame her, and eventually came up with what I considered a brilliant solution. Whenever Kay needed to use the makeshift bedpan, I stood nearby and made as much noise as I could by rustling some newspapers together. Sometimes we would get the giggles, making it harder for each of us to complete our tasks, and it was a great relief to both of us when Kay finally recovered.

Gradually we became accustomed to life in Tanforan, especially to standing in long lines for everything. We lined up to get into the mess hall or to use a laundry tub or to buy something at the canteen (finding only shoelaces when we got in) or to get into the occasional movies that were shown.

We got used to rushing back to our stall after dinner for the 6:00 P.M. head count (we were still in bed for the morning count), and to the sudden unexpected campwide searches for contraband by the FBI when we were confined to our stalls for several hours.

For diversion we could also go to talent shows, recorded concerts, discussion groups, Saturday night dances, softball games, art classes, and hobby shows exhibiting beautiful handicraft made by resourceful residents from scrap material.

Soon visitors from the outside were allowed to come in as far as the grandstand, and many of our friends came laden with cakes, fruit, candy, cookies, and news from the outside.

Representatives from the university, the YMCA and YWCA, and various church groups also came to give us their support and help. They were working on arrangements to get students out of camp and back into schools as soon as possible.

One day our neighbor Mrs. Harpainter came to see us, bringing all sorts of snacks along with flowers from her garden for Mama. Her boys, however, were not allowed inside because they were under sixteen.

When Kay and I heard they were waiting outside the gate, we hurried to the fence to talk to them.

"Teddy! Bobby!"

We ran to greet them, squeezing our fingers through the chain links to touch their hands.

But an armed guard quickly shouted, "Hey, you two! Get away from the fence!"

Kay and I stepped back immediately. We didn't want to tangle with anyone holding a gun. Bobby and Teddy watched us in total horror, and told us later that they thought we were going to be shot right before their eyes.

When my mother's good friend, Eleanor Knight, came to see us, we asked her to see how Laddie was getting along. Each day we wondered about him, but the boy who had promised to write hadn't even sent us a postcard. And then we learned why he had not written.

"I'm so sorry," Eleanor wrote, "but your dear Laddie died just a few weeks after you left Berkeley."

I was sure he had died of a broken heart, thinking we had abandoned him. I ran outside to find a place to cry, but there were people wherever I turned. I didn't want to see anybody, but there was no place to hide. There was no place to be alone—not in the latrine or the showers or anywhere in the entire camp.

After three months of communal living, I was tired of constantly seeing people and making idle conversation. All I wanted was to be alone in some quiet place and be anywhere but inside a prison camp. What I didn't know then was that getting out would mean going to a place far more cruel and unforgiving than Tanforan.

15
TOPAZ

I first heard the rumors in the showers.

"Did you know we're being sent to Idaho?"

"Really? I heard it was Utah."

Nobody really knew anything, but everyone passed on all the rumors they heard in the mess halls or the latrines or the laundry barracks.

Early in September we were finally informed that we would be sent to Topaz, the Central Utah Relocation Center near the town of Delta. It was time for our temporary city to wind down and close its recreation centers, its small mess halls, and all its schools.

Just when I was beginning to make some progress with the children in my class, it was time to say good-bye. We had a final program for the parents, cleaned out our school barracks, and watched the children scatter to their stable homes.

Once more we packed up our belongings, but this time my father was there to help us. He dismantled all the makeshift furniture our friends had made for us from scrap lumber and converted them into large crates. This time we were traveling far and needed something sturdier than our old canvas bundle.

Two days before our section of camp was scheduled to leave, we were instructed to stay in our quarters so our freight baggage could be inspected.

We waited all day for the inspectors, rushing through our meals to be back in our stalls before they came. Finally, about 4:00 P.M. they reached our stable.

"They're here!" I announced happily. But I had rejoiced too soon. When they reached the stall two doors away, they decided to stop for the day. It was like having the ice cream drop from your cone just when you'd opened your mouth for the first delicious bite. Now we would have to wait again for the inspectors the next day.

"Well, *shikataganai*," Papa said. "It can't be helped."

But I found it hard to be as patient. By this time I should have been used to waiting, but each new frustration made me want to go somewhere and scream at somebody. The trouble was, there was no one at whom I could scream.

On the day we were assigned to leave, friends came to help us get our bedding and larger bundles to the departure point. There our hand baggage was subjected to one last inspection. I wondered just what the army expected to find with their constant search and inspections, but they continued to search us as though we might all be smuggling contraband.

Once we were inspected, we were told to sit on the benches and wait. As time passed, children began to fidget and babies began to cry. Everyone was tired, but still we waited.

The train that was to take us to Utah had been pulled up to a siding at the rear of the camp. When it was finally time for us to board, we walked single file between a double row of military police and were counted as we climbed onto the train. It didn't look anything like the trains we had taken to go to Los Angeles.

"My gosh," Kay exclaimed. "Look at this train!"

It had fixtures for gaslights, and the seats were as hard and straight-backed as pews in an old church. The two Pullman cars at the rear were for the ill and disabled.

I thought it looked like something out of the nineteenth century, and Papa surmised they must have taken it out of storage.

We all gathered at the windows, looking out at the people left in Tanforan who would be following us later. They had rushed through supper to be at the fence to see us off, and I could see a few of my friends waving and calling to me.

As the train slowly began to move, we shouted back and forth, reluctant to be separated once again.

"So long! See you in Topaz! Good-bye! Take care!"

It was only a cluster of old stables and barracks, but it had been our only home in the world for five months. And now it was another wrench. This time we were leaving our home state of California for distant and unknown parts, and that made this new uprooting seem even more ominous.

Long after Tanforan was behind us, we contined to stare out the window, drinking in sights we had missed for five months. Houses, gardens, stores, cars, traffic lights, dogs, white children riding bicycles. All these ordinary things seemed so strange and wonderful to us. But soon it was dusk, and we were told the shades must be drawn from sunset to sunrise.

We reluctantly drew the shades, shutting out the world,

feeling more stifled than ever in our prison-train confinement.

"Kay, are you still up?" I whispered.

She groaned, squirming, as she tried to find a comfortable position in which to sleep.

I tried my mother next. "Mom, can you sleep?"

"I don't think anybody can," she sighed.

Only Papa, always relaxed, seemed to be taking short cat-naps. Most of the people in our car were stirring uncomfortably. Some walked up and down the aisle. Some drank water until the container was dry. Some got trainsick. Children were crying. Everyone waited restlessly for morning.

By noon the next day we were in Nevada sagebrush country. Suddenly, in the middle of an absolutely desolate stretch of desert, the train pulled to a stop. Our car captain announced that we could all get off for a thirty-minute break to stretch our legs.

"But don't go beyond the row of MPs," he warned.

Or what, I wondered. Would they shoot?

I saw the row of helmeted MPs lined up between our train and the desert, and wondered who would want to escape in this godforsaken patch of land. All any of us wanted was to stretch our sore muscles and breathe a little fresh air.

By the second night on the train, we were all so stiff and numb, sleep was out of the question. I could hardly wait to get to Utah.

About 9:30 P.M. we crossed the Great Salt Lake, and the car captain turned out the lights and allowed us to raise the blinds so we could look out.

I caught my breath at the sight of that magnificent lake shimmering in the moonlight. It looked so serene and majestic—a part of something so much greater than our small rickety prison train. It was as though we'd been given a few magical moments from the earth, as a gift, to carry in our hearts into the concentration camp.

When we reached the Salt Lake City station, we quickly opened the windows to catch a glimpse of the "real world." It felt good to hear the busy normal sounds of the station and the calls of the men who were servicing our train.

As I thrust my head out the window to take it all in, I was astonished to see a familiar face. It was one of my former Nisei classmates from the university.

"Helen! What in the world are you doing here?" I asked.

She told me she had evacuated voluntarily, moving out of the restricted zone before the uprooting, and was now living in Salt Lake City. "When I heard the internee train was coming through," she explained, "I came to see if I could find anybody I knew."

She was anxious to know what had happened to other friends in our class.

"They're scattered everywhere," I told her, "in camps all over the United States."

We talked as fast as we could, exchanging news of what had happened to each of us since we last spoke on campus. And then it was time for the train to leave. She took my hand briefly.

"Good luck, Yo."

"Thanks," I said, "I think I'll need it."

I waved to her as the train slowly pulled out of the station, thinking how lucky she was. She was free to return to her own home and live like a normal person. But I was still a prisoner, simply because I had not been able to evacuate voluntarily as she had. It didn't make sense. I was filled with envy as I leaned back on the hard seat and tried to get some sleep.

We finally reached Delta, Utah, the next morning. I was so anxious to get off the train, I didn't even mind being counted again as we filed off. For the last leg of our journey to Topaz, we were transferred to buses.

The scenery outside looked encouraging, for I saw many small farms and cultivated fields.

"Maybe it won't be so bad out there," I said hopefully.

But Kay just said, "Don't get your hopes up too soon, Yo."

And she was right. We had only ridden for about a half hour when there was a sudden change of scenery. There were no more trees or fields or vegetation of any kind.

Soon all we could see were dry clumps of greasewood. We were entering the edge of the Sevier Desert fifteen miles east of Delta, and the surroundings now were as bleak as a bleached bone.

The bus made a sudden turn into the heart of the sun-drenched desert, and there, in the middle of nowhere, were rows and rows of tar-papered barracks. They looked like small match boxes laid out neatly on a vast white table.

This was Topaz, one of ten such concentration camps in which Japanese Americans were interned throughout the United States. All of them were in equally barren and isolated areas and were operated by a civilian agency called the War Relocation Authority.

Earlier arrivals had organized a small group to welcome us to our new home, and the Boy Scout Drum and Bugle Corps played bravely in the blazing sun. They were holding signs that read, "Welcome to Topaz."

A few of our friends were there to meet us as well, looking as though they'd just crawled out of a barrel of flour. They were covered with dust, but they smiled and tried to look cheerful.

"We'll help you get settled," they offered, and walked with us to Block 7, Barrack 2, Apartment C, to which we had been assigned.

The camp was a one-mile square area, surrounded by a barbed-wire fence, with guard towers at each of its four corners. There were forty-two blocks in all, each block containing twelve barracks, and in the center, a mess hall, a latrine-washroom, and a laundry barrack. With eight thousand residents, Topaz became the fifth largest city in Utah.

The army, in its haste to construct this camp, had removed everything that grew in this once peaceful lake bed and churned it into one big mass of loose powdery dust.

Block 7 was in the northeast corner of camp, and as we plodded along, we created swirls of dust that sifted into our eyes, mouths, noses, and lungs with each step.

After two sleepless nights on the train, the glaring white sand and the altitude made me feel strangely light-headed. I felt as though I just wanted to lie down in the sand and go to sleep.

We were worried about Mama. "Are you all right?" we asked.

She nodded silently, holding a handkerchief over her nose and mouth. Her hair and eyelashes were covered with dust, just as ours were.

When we reached Block 7, we found that each barrack was divided into six rooms. Our room, about eighteen feet by twenty feet, was in the center, for families of four or more. There was nothing in it except for four army cots folded on the floor.

Because the interior sheetrock walls had not yet been installed, dust was seeping in steadily from all the cracks in the siding and around the windows. The room was smoky with dust and the floor was covered with it. We were speechless.

Papa quickly found a broom and swept out the room, while Kay and I went to check out the facilities. We discovered that the toilets had no seats, the laundry room had no water, and there were no lights in the showers or the latrines.

Our water was pumped from nearby artesian wells, and twice during our first day, it was turned off completely. We soon learned to keep our kettle filled at all times, but there was no way we could plan ahead for showers or laundry. We just had to rely on luck for those.

Although we were still wobbly from the long train ride, we went to the mess hall to have some lunch. The food was so meager, the Issei cook came out to apologize.

"We wanted to welcome you with better fare," he said, as though it were his fault, "but we just don't have the provisions. We're so sorry."

The camp was in short supply of everything, and nothing was ready. We wondered why the War Relocation Authority couldn't have waited to bring us in until the camp was completed and fully equipped. But apparently the WRA had its own agenda, which we couldn't begin to fathom.

At that moment all we longed for was some rest. We were so exhausted, we set up the cots in our dusty room and fell asleep on the springs without waiting for the mattresses to arrive.

16
DUST
STORM

"It's time to get up! Better hurry!"

It was a familiar call from Mama, but for a minute I couldn't remember where I was. Then I heard the cook banging on a dishpan, calling our block to breakfast.

My feet were cold and my nose felt icy. It was no wonder. When I got up, I found a thin layer of ice on top of the water in our kettle. We had been issued a potbellied stove, but it wasn't doing us any good. Like everyone else's, it was sitting outside, covered with dust, waiting for the work crews to come install it.

Coming as we did from the mild climate of California, none of us felt well in the desert. Mornings began with freezing temperatures, and afternoons soared into the eighties and nineties. The altitude (4,600 feet above sea level) made us light-headed, and lack of proper refrigeration for our food brought about an immediate rash of food poisoning.

The latrines were soon in such an unspeakable state of filth, I had nightmares about them for years afterward. But Papa, with his usual energy and civic-mindedness, rounded up three other men and spent all of his first morning in Topaz cleaning the latrines in our block.

In the afternoon he discovered ice-cream bars at the canteen and bought several boxes for the Boy Scouts who were marching again in the blazing sun to greet new arrivals.

Wanting to do something useful myself, I volunteered to work as secretary to our newly elected block manager. The poor man spent all his time trying to placate disgruntled residents, since no one was happy about his housing assignment. Everybody wanted to move elsewhere.

What people didn't realize was that no matter where they moved in Topaz, they would find the same frustrating conditions. Barren unfinished rooms. Dust everywhere. Sudden water stoppages.

Those of us in Block 7 were relatively lucky. Later arrivals from Tanforan were sent to barracks with gaping holes in the roof where the stovepipe was to go. Others went to barracks where the roof was still being tarred, and one woman suffered second-degree burns on her face when boiling tar seeped onto the bed where she was sleeping.

Those who arrived even later had no barracks at all to go to and slept on cots placed in laundry barracks or in the corridors of the hospital.

About a week after we arrived, I encountered my first dust storm. As the afternoon temperatures began to rise, I felt a hot, dry wind and saw murky gray clouds gathering in the sky.

I was walking home with a friend when the wind suddenly became a fierce, ominous living thing, twisting and shrieking and howling at us as though we had incurred its wrath. It flung swirling masses of sand into the air, engulfing us in such thick clouds of dust, we couldn't even see barracks ten feet away.

We ran into the nearest laundry barrack and found the air inside already thick with dust. The flimsy barrack shuddered with each blast of wind, and we heard garbage cans and wooden crates slamming against the building as the wind flung them through the air.

We crouched near the washtubs for over an hour, waiting for the wind to subside even a little. When it did, we decided to make a run for our homes.

"Be careful, Yo," my friend called.

"I will. You, too."

We separated then, and I staggered alone through the billowing dust, weaving as though I were drunk, blown this way and that by the howling wind. Sand blew into my eyes, so I could barely see. It blew into my nose and mouth, so I could hardly breathe. The dust was making me choke, but fear of being swept off my feet and flung into the desert kept me going.

When I finally stumbled into our room, I was covered with dust. It was in my hair and on my eyelashes and in my nose. My mouth tasted like chalk. I found Mama sitting alone, worrying about the rest of us.

"Oh, Yo Chan, I'm so glad you're safe," she said, hugging me.

We were worried about Kay and Papa, but there was nothing we could do. We simply covered everything with newspapers and lay on our cots, our faces covered with towels, waiting for the storm to end.

Kay and Papa came home about supper time, covered with dust from head to toe. They had both been caught too far away to run home as I had, but they were safe.

By sunset the storm had spent itself. When I went outside to look up at the wide encircling desert sky, it had turned glorious shades of pink and gold and lavender. It was hard to believe it was the same sky that only a few hours earlier had spewed out such suffocating terror. It was almost as though the dust storm had never happened, but I knew from our dust-filled room that it had indeed been quite real.

As with many others, life in the desert didn't agree with Kay, and once again she had a long sick spell. This time her major problem proved to be my parents' well-meaning Issei friends who wanted to be helpful.

There was no place for any of us to hide. Kay was at the mercy of anyone who came to call, even if she was behind the monk's-cloth curtains made by Mama to separate our cots from the living area.

One day Mrs. Tana brought her a broth that she claimed could cure any ailment.

"Please try it, Keiko San," she urged. "I know it will make you well."

With Mrs. Tana sitting beside her waiting, Kay couldn't refuse, so she drank it reluctantly. It wasn't exactly a magic cure, but Kay did get better in about a week. The next time she saw Mrs. Tana, the lady beamed happily.

"Ah, Keiko San, you're well now," she said. "I knew my earthworm brew would cure you."

"Your what?" Kay hoped she hadn't heard correctly.

"My boiled earthworm broth," Mrs. Tana explained. "I've never found it to fail."

After that, Kay could never be persuaded to try anyone's homemade remedies. And it was Mama, always looking for ways to improve her health, who obligingly tried the oily black essence of egg yolk that Mrs. Tana brought next.

"It will give you endless and unlimited energy," she assured my mother. But, unfortunately, the smelly black oil didn't work.

17
SCHOOL IN THE DESERT

Whenever we heard someone shout, "The water's running!" we would grab our laundry and rush for the tubs. By the time we hand-washed sheets, towels, and clothing for the four of us, we were too exhausted to do anything else.

In the early days we seemed to spend most of our time sweeping dust from our room or doing our laundry. But we soon saw the need for Topaz to be organized and begin functioning as a community.

My father served on many committees and was also elected chairman of the board of directors of the canteen, which, at the government's suggestion, was converted into a consumers' cooperative. He was also appointed president of the Cooperative Congress and was as busy now as he had ever been back in Berkeley.

Kay and her Mills colleague again organized the nursery schools, and I signed up to teach in the elementary schools. Mama, as always, created a home for us in our small dusty room, spending much of her time knitting or sewing with material ordered by mail.

Two elementary schools were opened, one in Block 8 near the administration building (to which all the white teachers employed by the WRA were assigned), and the other in Block 41 at the far end of camp.

I was assigned to teach the second grade in Block 41. Eager to get back to teaching, I hurried to Block 41 to inspect my classroom, but was greeted by a shocking sight. Not only was there a gaping hole in the roof, there were no interior sheetrock walls, no tables or chairs or books or teaching supplies of any kind.

The only object in the room was a potbellied coal stove that had yet to be connected.

I didn't see how the schools could possibly open, but registration proceeded as scheduled. The children came in great numbers, and we registered them in a barrack as cold as the inside of a refrigerator. We tried moving outside into the feeble morning sun, but even the sight of sunlight scarcely made a difference.

I expected to be notified before Monday that school openings would be postponed. But hearing nothing, I bundled up in my winter coat, gloves, boots, and a heavy scarf, and set off for Block 41.

Many children in my class were already there, shivering and huddling pathetically around the cold unusable stove.

"Maybe we'll get warm if we sing and clap our hands," I suggested. But it was so cold our breath left little wisps of steam in the icy air, and we could not stop shivering.

Not wanting to risk their health, I finally decided to send the children home, but I knew they were just as disappointed as I was.

Finally, after meeting with the school administrators, we decided to hold our teachers' meetings in the morning and teach in the afternoon when the sun had warmed our classrooms. That solved one problem, but we still had to contend with the dust that blew in from the rooftop hole in all the rooms.

One afternoon, just as I was starting my class, I heard the dread sound of the wailing wind. Soon dust poured into the room as though someone were pouring bucketfuls through the hole in our roof.

We knew the classroom was no place to wait out the storm, and following a quick consultation among the teachers, we all sent our children home.

"Be careful!" I called as I watched the children disappear into walls of dust.

They looked so small and the storm was so big. It was hardly a fair match. I could do nothing, however, but run home myself, stopping every few feet to catch my breath.

I worried all afternoon about the children, but sending them home proved to be a wise decision, for the storm grew steadily worse and lasted late into the night.

In spite of the storm, Papa had gone out to an urgent meeting, but Mama, Kay, and I were in our room. The wind rattled our barrack like a wild beast wanting to devour us, crunching us up like so many dried bones.

I had often seen my mother pray, her head bowed, her hands clasped. Always it seemed to be a nice quiet conversation with God. But that night it was different. She was kneeling beside her bed, beseeching God to keep us safe. And seeing her, I was filled with a sense of total helplessness.

Papa got home safely, and all the barracks survived the storm, but the camp's chicken coops were blown into the desert along with their hapless occupants.

I dreaded those dust storms more than anything I have

encountered in my life, but we had many more before I left Topaz. Even today the mere thought of them churns me up inside.

In spite of all the hardships, our schools somehow stumbled along, and we had our share of little adventures. One day I got permission to take my class outside the camp-grounds to visit a nearby sheepherder. It felt good to walk out beyond the barbed-wire fence, even though it was only to see some scraggly, unkempt sheep, and the children seemed genuinely happy.

Another day I almost came totally unglued when a snake found its way into my classroom. I have always hated things that slithered and crawled, and I also feared the deadly scorpions that abounded in the desert. Not wanting to show my fear to the children, however, I managed somehow to keep the class going until recess.

Then I quickly ran for help and found a braver teacher who carried the snake back into the desert with a big stick. "I think it was quite harmless," she said calmly, but was kind enough to whisper the words into my ear.

I had an easier time dealing with the pet fish that one of the parents brought back from a distant river. He had gone out with a work crew to gather pebbles for the roads, and his son brought the fish to class in an old mayonnaise jar.

The children named it Percy and loved it dearly. But Percy must have missed its river home, for one morning we found the fish floating lifeless in its glass prison. I was sorry we hadn't let it live out its life swimming freely as it should have, and I helped the children bury Percy in the sand just outside our classroom door.

In November we made a small Pilgrim village from old milk cartons in preparation for Thanksgiving. But by then a series of dust storms, rain squalls, and a severe snowstorm finally brought our limping school system to a complete halt. It was a wonder to me that we had managed to stay open as long as we had.

The schools, it was announced, would remain closed until all interior sheetrock walls and stoves could be installed, as they had been in our home barracks.

Thank goodness, I thought. But if the children could have had their way, they probably would have elected to keep the schools open. Going to school, after all, was the one thing that most closely resembled their lives back in California.

18
CONCENTRATION CAMP CHRISTMAS

The day before Christmas a large carton of greens arrived for my mother from her friends in Connecticut. Opening it was like opening a door to an evergreen forest. It smelled glorious. It was the smell of Christmas.

"Ah, *ureshii!*" Mama exclaimed, as she buried her face in the greenery.

I hadn't seen her so happy in a long time. She kept only two or three sprays, and immediately made a list of friends with whom she wanted to share the rest. Eager to distribute the fragrant branches, she and my father left immediately, laden with Christmas in their arms.

Watching them go, I remembered those early days of my life when we would receive a crate of juicy Sunkist oranges from my uncle or a box of sweet seedless grapes from our Livingston friends.

The first thing Mama did was to send me over to both neighbors with a big bag of fruit for each of them. She and Papa would then think of all the other friends with whom they wanted to share the fruit.

Keiko and I would watch the dwindling fruit in dismay and plead, "Don't give it *all* away, Mama. Leave some for *us!*"

It took a long time for us to learn that our parents derived more pleasure from sharing their bounty than from enjoying it themselves. But we weren't able to feel quite as generous. We still had to say, "Leave some for *us!*"

That night, as I lay on my cot, surrounded by the fragrance of the fir sprays, listening to Christmas carols on the radio, I thought about how we would spend Christmas Day in a concentration camp.

We would go to church, we would visit friends, and we would have a special turkey dinner at the mess hall without having to stand in line. As they had on Thanksgiving, the mess hall crew would serve us at our tables as a special treat.

The turkey itself would be a rare and welcome change from our usual dull fare, which often included catfish. (I still can't eat it today). Our daily food budget was thirty-nine cents per person, and, of course, we were subject to the same wartime rationing restrictions that applied outside of camp.

When I was a child, I did the same thing on Christmas Eve. I would lie in bed and think about all the wonderful things I would do on Christmas Day.

It would start very early while it was still dark. Keiko and I would leap out of bed and run to the fireplace where we had hung our long, white cotton stockings. The living room would be icy cold and the air filled with the sweet tingly smell of the Christmas tree by the window.

We would stand there shivering, looking at all the glittery ornaments and the shimmery silver tinsel and the pile of gifts beneath the tree. But soon we grabbed our lumpy stockings and ran back to the warmth of our beds, emptying everything out on top.

There would always be an orange in the toe, then Hershey bars and maybe a tiny Kewpie doll, or a top, or jacks and a ball, or puzzles, or, one year, a harmonica. I knew it was Mama who filled my stocking, but the joy of finding the little surprises tumble out of my stocking was too delicious to give up, and I continued to hang one up for a long time.

In those days the high point of Christmas Day was the Sunday School program at church in the evening. For weeks each class practiced a play or a song or a recitation. Nobody ever got anything right, and the teachers would be frantic. But when they pulled open the sagging bed-sheet curtain on Christmas night, we would perform as we never had during rehearsals, much to the relief of all concerned.

After the program, Santa Claus (often my father, since he was just the right shape) would come out calling, "Meeeerry Christmas!" as he rang the big black Sunday School bell. We would all reach eagerly for the boxes of hard Christmas candy he carried in his pillowcase sack, and our Sunday School teachers would have presents for us as well. I never liked the flat square boxes that meant boring handkerchiefs, but sometimes I was pleasantly surprised.

When Christmas and New Year's were over in Topaz, there was nothing left to look forward to. Work crews had gone out in the fall to a distant river, bringing back small saplings that were planted along the wide firebreaks between blocks. Each block was also given a tree to plant in front of its mess hall.

Everyone was hoping for the emergence of swelling buds to signal a green, leafy spring. But the saplings never had a chance in the alkaline soil of Topaz. Covered with winter's ice, they soon became no more than crystalline skeletons, and the children finished them off by playing leapfrog over them as they walked to school.

Then the shooting took place. One evening about dusk, an old man hunting arrowheads near the camp's southern border was shot to death by a sentry in the guard tower.

"I ordered him to halt," the guard explained, "but he tried to crawl under the fence."

The old man's body, however, was found a good three feet inside the fence, and it was possible he had not heard the guard's order from high up in the tower.

The death caused an uproar in camp. People were enraged that the MP had killed an innocent man.

"Why did he have to shoot to kill? Why didn't he fire a warning shot?"

"Next time it could be a child, for god's sake!"

The entire camp was in turmoil, and a campwide funeral was held for the old man. His casket was covered with crepe paper flowers made by the camp's women, and he was buried in the desert because there was no room for a cemetery inside the fence. It seemed such a cruel irony that he could finally get beyond the barbed-wire fence only because he had died.

It saddened me to think of anyone being buried in the vast, lonely desert. Already there were three other graves out there—one of them belonging to the father of one of my friends.

I sometimes thought about the little cemetery—not during the terrifying dust storms—but in the evenings when we took walks to watch the sunsets that filled the vast sky with soft magical colors. Or at night when I saw what appeared to be millions of sparkling stars scattered over an enormous endless blackness.

I knew then that the desert had its own particular peace and solace. And I hoped those who lay beneath its skies were now embraced by that same unending peace.

The bleakness of Topaz was now seeping deep inside me. I tried to keep busy. I worked hard at school and faithfully attended all the teachers' meetings and seminars. I wrote to friends scattered in concentration camps all over the United States. They had addresses such as 42-2-A, Jerome, Arkansas, or 60-2-B, Poston, Arizona. My grandmother and cousins now lived in Block 30, Barrack 10, Apt. A, Heart Mountain, Wyoming.

I learned how to knit. I went to art classes. I read every book I could find. I sang in the church choir. I played cards or went to an occasional movie at the canteen with my friends. I went to birthday parties and even to a wedding.

I had an impacted wisdom tooth removed. I caught one cold after another. I fell on the unpaved roads. I lost my voice from the dust. I was tired of having people around me constantly. And I was homesick for Berkeley.

I felt as though I couldn't bear being locked up one more day. I wanted to go out into the world and live a real life.

In Tanforan, I had passed up a chance to go out to Smith College because I couldn't bear to leave my family and friends behind living in horse stalls. I wanted to stay and do what I could to help.

But now many of our friends were leaving for the outside. Both Kay and I needed to get out as well, and our parents encouraged us to get on with our lives.

Qualified citizens who had a place to go and means of supporting themselves were permitted to leave if they would not endanger national security or cause a disturbance in the community. I certainly wasn't dangerous, and I didn't intend to cause a disturbance anywhere.

Kay and I filled out dozens of forms and wrote a barrage of letters to the National Japanese Student Relocation Council. Organized by the Quakers, this group helped hundreds of students leave camp and return to school.

We wrote so many letters, the people with whom we corresponded began to seem like old friends. But they could only locate a school for us. We couldn't leave camp until we got clearance from the government, and that was not such a simple matter.

In March 1943, there was a logjam of hundreds of requests for leave clearance, and the government was working, as usual, in its slow, cumbersome fashion.

We took our place in a long invisible line, waiting. And we tried to be patient.

19

VOLUNTEERS FROM BEHIND BARBED WIRE

One day our school supervisor got permission to take four teachers out to visit an elementary school in Delta, and I was one of the lucky ones. Except for the brief visit to the sheep farm, I had not been outside the gate since the day we arrived, and I could hardly wait to go.

I felt a bit nervous as our car approached the gate.

"How many?" the guard asked the driver.

The teachers were Japanese Americans. The driver and the supervisor were white.

"Six, including Caucasians," the driver answered.

The guard peered in to inspect us. "Which one is Mrs. Caucasians?" he asked warily.

I realized we had nothing to fear from this guard and leaned back to enjoy the outing as the guard waved us through.

Delta was small, but it was a real honest-to-goodness town with paved streets, lights, cars, stores, and restaurants. It was amazing how distanced we had become from the outside world during our incarceration.

"Look! There's a five-and-ten!"

"And a restaurant! And so many *hakujin* (white people)!"

We were like children let loose in a toy store, hardly knowing which way to look for fear we'd miss something.

I was so impressed with the professional teacher whose class we visited, I came away with pages of notes. But the best part of the day was our lunch at the Southern Hotel, with its linen-covered tables, shiny silverware, and something we hadn't seen for many months—menus. Not having made choices about our food for so long, it was hard to resist ordering everything.

We didn't dare linger too long over lunch, however, since we wanted to leave time for shopping at the five-and-ten. We spent fifteen glorious minutes in a frantic shopping frenzy and came out feeling positively uplifted.

That brief taste of the outside world reminded me just how deprived we were in camp. I felt exhilarated for a few days after our outing, but soon wound down like a tired clock. Quickly overcome once more by our dreary life in Topaz, I was more anxious than ever to be free.

The same feelings of restlessness and frustration were spreading throughout camp like a disease. Isolated and imprisoned, we had lost our dignity as human beings. Having also lost control of our own lives and destiny, we couldn't help but feel depressed and helpless.

Topaz had its share of disgruntled and violent people, and before long their anger burst out in ugly incidents. I was afraid to walk alone after dark, and it became dangerous for my father as well. There were those who focused their anger and resentment at community leaders such as my father, who worked closely with the white adminstration, and several men were attacked and beaten as they walked alone at night.

There were also those who felt the co-op wasn't being run properly. They blamed my father for its shortcomings and came to our room to voice their complaints.

I had never before heard anyone shout at my father with such hostility. I was frightened and angered by their crude language and tried to think of some way to keep those men from returning.

Then I recalled the artist in our stable at Tanforan. Desperate for some privacy, she had hung a large quarantine sign on her door to keep visitors out. When her friends banged on her stall door asking what ailed her, she simply shouted, "Hoof-and-mouth disease! Go away!"

I thought that device might work for us as well and made a big quarantine sign, which I tacked on our door.

"That ought to keep those thugs away," I said to Papa.

But early the next morning, friends and neighbors came knocking at our door.

"Who is sick, Uchida San?"

"What is the problem? Is it mumps? Or measles?

"Are you all right? Can we help?"

Unfortunately, Papa couldn't be like the artist. "I'm sorry," he apologized. "It was a mistake. We're all fine." And he quickly removed my sign.

I felt as though our home, which had always welcomed so many friends, was now being invaded by those who meant us harm. I was apprehensive, but there was nothing I could do about it.

To add to the general discontent, recruiters from the U.S. Army appeared in all the concentration camps with a bombshell issue.

Until then, Nisei men could not enlist in the army even if they'd wanted to. They had been classified IV-C (not acceptable for service because of ancestry).

The secretary of war, however, had had a change of heart and the ruling was reversed. Furthermore, the army now wanted Japanese American men to volunteer for a segregated all-Nisei combat team, which they claimed would gain special attention and allow the Nisei to prove their loyalty in a dramatic and forceful way.

But the Nisei men wondered why they couldn't serve as any other American.

"Why should we be singled out when there are no all-German or all-Italian units?" they asked.

"We may just become cannon fodder to be sent to the most dangerous zones!"

The Issei parents had their own questions.

"How can a country that has deprived our sons of their civil rights now ask them to volunteer their lives from behind barbed wire? Something is wrong here."

Jimmy and Walt were two eighteen year olds whom Kay had once taught in her Sunday School class. They had been among the church friends who came to help us pack when we left Berkeley, and we thought of them somewhat as kid brothers. Now they came to tell us they were thinking of volunteering.

The army had told them that by volunteering they could help determine the future of the Nisei in America. That seemed a terrible burden to put on their young shoulders, I thought. Why should they have to prove the loyalty of the Nisei with such a tremendous sacrifice?

The War Relocation Authority made matters worse by requiring a mass campwide registration at the same time. Included in their questionnaire was a statement forswearing allegiance to the emperor of Japan, which we were all asked to sign.

115

But how could we Nisei forswear a loyalty we never had and sign a statement that implied we'd had such an allegiance before signing it?

And how could our Issei parents sign it? They were ineligible for American citizenship by law, so had no choice but to remain Japanese citizens. If they gave that up as well, they would be stateless.

It was an impossible situation, and the camp was in an uproar. The army and the WRA eventually realized they had made a mistake and revised their questionnaire. But only after they had caused untold turmoil and anguish in all the camps.

Under these conditions, there were many young men who understandably refused to sign the statement or to volunteer for a segregated unit while they and their families remained in prison camps. It took courage for them to say no and to stand up for their civil rights.

It also took courage to say yes. Jimmy and Walt were among those who decided to volunteer and came one day to say good-bye to us.

"We're volunteering to prove we're as good as any other American," they said. "And maybe we'll all have a better future for it."

We went to see them off at the gate when the volunteers left for basic training. They looked so young and eager and brave and sad. I cried as I watched them waving from the bus window, wondering if we would ever see them again.

Some of my classmates from Cal had also volunteered from other camps, and two of them never returned. There were many gold star mothers in the concentration camps of America, and their gold stars, indicating the loss of a son in the war, hung proudly in the dusty windows of their barracks.

The magnificent records of the All-Nisei 442nd Regimen-

116

tal Combat Team and the 100th Infantry Battalion are now well known. They were among the most decorated units of the entire army, and they gave us a history of which we could all be proud. They more than proved their loyalty with their courage and their heroic achievements. They truly *did* help make a better future for all the Japanese Americans in America.

20
BACK TO THE REAL WORLD

Spring came slowly to Topaz with a gentle softness in the air. It also came for me in the sky and in a tin can.

When my mother's friend, Louise DeForest, had sent me cupcakes with frosting and candles for my November birthday, she had also sent me a daffodil bulb. I planted it in a tin can from the mess hall and watched it like a mother bird guarding her eggs.

The day I discovered a small bud swelling between the tall green leaves, the seagulls came from nowhere like a second miracle. I heard their cries and rushed to the door. And there they were, winging their way toward the west. They were the first birds I had seen in the desert.

"Hey, everybody! Come look!" I shouted.

I had no idea where they had come from or where they were going. Maybe, I thought, they would keep right on flying until they reached San Francisco Bay. I imagined them coming to rest on the old pilings at the pier, sniffing the damp salt air and swooping down to the water for a tasty shrimp.

"Hey, you lucky seagulls," I called to them. "Fly safe!"

I watched them soar with easy grace over our desert until they disappeared over the mountains.

It seemed I'd had two lucky omens. My daffodil was about to bloom and I had seen the seagulls. Spring was coming, and maybe, I thought, I would be getting out of camp soon.

Good news came first for my sister early in May. She was offered a job as assistant in the Department of Education's Nursery School at Mt. Holyoke College in Massachusetts. She was also invited to spend the summer at a Quaker Study Center.

Soon after, my own good news arrived. I was awarded a full graduate fellowship in the Department of Education at Smith College. It was exactly what I'd hoped for. And for the summer I was invited to live with my friend, Cathy Sellew, and her parents in Brooklyn. We had corresponded ever since we'd met as children in Cornwall, Connecticut, and now our lives were coming together again, like the spinning together of two strands of thread. My mother had begun her friendships so long ago in Japan, and now Cathy and I were weaving our own strands into the same tapestry. It all seemed part of a master plan that provided a home for me to go to from the Utah desert.

Kay and I would be going to colleges in the same area and would be able to see each other often. Everything was working out better than we could have imagined. Now we had only to wait for our indefinite leave papers.

One morning as I was teaching my class, I was surprised by my father, who came in waving a piece of paper.

"Good news, Yo!" he called. "Your leave clearance has come! So has Kay's!"

Knowing how anxiously I waited for that clearance, he had rushed all the way to my school to bring me the news. The long wait was over. With all our papers in order, Kay and I could leave Topaz at last.

On my last day at school, the children of my class gave me a little clay bowl that one of them had made. Then, standing together, giggling and squirming, they sang one last song for me.

"I'll never forget you," I told them fondly. "I'll be sure to write."

On our last Sunday in camp, Kay and I went to say good-bye to all our friends, especially the older Issei who would have to remain in camp until the war ended. We went first to see the Wasas, now grown as thin and frail as dried weeds in the sun.

"How wonderful that you are going out," they said, so pleased for us. Unable to bake a sweet treat for me as she used to do so long ago, Mrs. Wasa just held me close and told me she would think of me every day.

It was hard to leave our parents and friends behind in the desolation of camp. But all Mama and Papa wanted was for us to be free.

"Don't worry about us," they said. "We're going to be all right. It's time now for you girls to go out and create new lives for yourselves."

Our parents wanted us to look ahead, not backward at what we had endured. They didn't want us to destroy our lives with bitterness that could fester inside us like a wound. They told us all this not so much with words as with the way they had lived their lives through this terrible ordeal.

The Issei lost everything they had worked so hard for

over so many years. But in spite of the loss and the humiliation, most of them remained steadfast and strong in spirit.

My parents had been caring and compassionate people before they were uprooted, and they still were. They never stopped helping others or creating a loving home for us no matter where we were.

I understood all this only many years after the war was over. On that warm, dusty day when we left Topaz, my thoughts were still too muddled for me to be properly grateful.

I wore a beige wool suit my mother had made for me, shoes I had ordered by mail, and a hat that came out of the trunk we'd sent for.

Many of our friends came with my parents to the gate to see us off, but at that moment I felt no joy in leaving. I cried as I hugged Mama and Papa and each of my friends.

There had been too many good-byes and separations, and this one seemed the hardest of all. I wanted so much to take them all out with me beyond the barbed wire. I wanted so much for them to be free, too.

I was glad to have Kay at my side as I climbed onto the small bus that would take us to Delta. From there we would catch our train to the East Coast. The desert sun was hot and the air was hazy with dust. I opened the bus window and leaned out, trying to smile.

And then it was time to go. The bus gave a lurch as it started down the rough unpaved road, and I looked back, waving as long as I could. I waved until my mother and father were just two small blurs in the cluster of people at the gate, but I could tell they were still waving their white handkerchiefs.

Then, finally, I turned around to face the road ahead. Kay and I were actually on our way back into the real world. We were free at last.

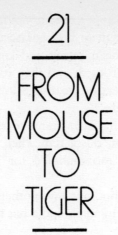

21

FROM
MOUSE
TO
TIGER

"Cathy?"

"Yoshi?"

It was as though we were meeting for the first time. Cathy and I had not seen each other for more than ten years. Now she was a tall, beautiful redhead, and I felt like an awkward child with the dust of Topaz still clinging to my shoes.

But Cathy and her parents welcomed me warmly and did their best to make me feel at home. After the crude environment of camp, life in their spacious three-bedroom apartment seemed elegant and full of grace.

In those days before TV dominated our lives, we sat together after dinner and talked about the day's events or the books each of us was reading. There was a large Webster's dictionary on a stand nearby, and Cathy's father would often look up the roots and meanings of unfamiliar words. It was a civilized life such as I had not known for many months.

Cathy had just begun working in Manhattan, and I, too, found a secretarial job for the summer in the offices of the Board of Presbyterian Churches on Fifth Avenue. This was my first job outside of camp, and my $40-a-week salary seemed a true windfall after my salary of $19 a month in Topaz.

I enjoyed my work, and the five women in my office took good care of me. But I could have done without the noon prayer meetings for the entire staff that I felt obliged to attend now and then. I tried to be properly pious, but more often than not, I would find myself thinking about what I was going to have for lunch as soon as I got out.

On weekends I often went with Cathy and her parents to their summer home in Cornwall. After the harsh bleakness of the desert, the vast green lawns and the lush forests were like an endless feast after a year of famine. I gulped in great breaths of green and couldn't get enough of it.

Before I left for Northampton in the fall, Cathy's mother went with me to buy a new warm coat for the New England winter, and I was ready to face Smith College.

The train ride to Northhampton, Massachusetts, was shorter and less tiring than the long ride from Utah on trains crowded with servicemen. But this time I didn't have Kay along for support or company. Now I was truly on my own.

When the conductor came to collect my ticket, he stared hard at me. "Say, you'd better not be a Jap," he threatened, scowling, "or I'll throw you off the train."

I stared back at him, not knowing what to say, and decided to say nothing. Fortunately, I didn't tell him what I thought of him, or I might have ended up in some train station halfway to Massachusetts and never gotten to Smith at all.

Smith College was as compact and tidy as the University of California was enormous and sprawling. At Cal, my Economics 1A class met in an eight-hundred-seat auditorium where the professor lectured from a podium on stage. He never would have known me if I were to bump into him outside the classroom.

At Smith, on the other hand, there were never more than six or seven students in my graduate classes, and in one there were only four of us. I was petrified. Instead of being an anonymous mouse sitting quietly, taking notes, I had to be a tiger and participate in discussions.

For the first month or two, I was in a state of near panic. But I managed to get an "A—Almost Distinction" grade on my educational psychology paper (which meant I'd almost gotten better than an A+), and learned to speak up in class now and then.

I lived with a dozen women from all parts of the United States and Canada in the Graduate House, and although I was the only Asian, none of them treated me differently because I looked like the enemy.

The best part of my school year was the two-week period of practice teaching at a public school in nearby Springfield. I discovered that the sixth graders were bigger than I, but fortunately, my assignment was with the first-grade class.

I was amazed at the skill of the teacher and watched every move she made. I also noticed that the letters she printed on the blackboard were about four inches high.

When it was my day to take over the class, I was careful to print enormous letters on the blackboard and talked to the children as though they were hearing-impaired. To my amazement, they listened quietly, did just as I asked, and not one of them ran from the room.

"You did just fine," the teacher assured me. "You're going to be a fine teacher. I can tell."

On my last day at the school, they presented me with a bouquet of flowers, and I gave the school some bells for their bell collection. The affection I felt for the children there was returned to me manyfold.

In May 1944, I received my master's degree in education from Smith College. This time I marched with my classmates in a cap and gown, and my diploma was handed to me by the president of the college. I felt as though I'd finally had the commencement I'd missed in Berkeley.

On the same day, the great black singer Marian Anderson was given an honorary degree, and I had my picture taken with her. It was a proud day for me, and I was happy Kay could be there to share it with me. I wished my parents could have been there as well.

They had finally gotten clearance to leave Topaz because of increasing violence and threats against my father and other community leaders. The co-op workers and all their church friends gave them a tremendous send-off, and they moved to Salt Lake City, where my father had a sponsor, to live in a small two-room apartment.

With my master's degree in hand, I applied for a teaching position, wondering if anyone would hire me. And then a letter came from a small Quaker school offering me a job.

The Quakers, who had given us so much help and support throughout the entire uprooting, were now offering me my first real job. I was to teach the first and second grades at Frankford Friends School, on the outskirts of Philadelphia, beginning in September. About the same time, one of my cousins became the first Japanese American teacher appointed to the Los Angeles County School System. It was a wonderful achievement.

I packed up my belongings once more, left Smith College, and headed for Philadelphia with my sister, who was spending the summer with me. I was ready and eager to become a teacher and to begin a new life.

22

GOOD MORNING, BOYS AND GIRLS

Every evening Kay and I returned to the hostel for Japanese Americans after spending the day in search of an apartment.

"Did you find anything today?" Mrs. Ino would ask.

"Not yet," we would answer.

Mrs. Ino and her husband ran the hostel in Philadelphia for people like us, just out of camp, looking for jobs and homes. Fortunately, I had a job. But we needed an apartment so we could send for our parents in Salt Lake City.

It was often dark by the time we returned to the hostel. I would see the lighted windows in the houses lining the streets and think of the people who had warm, lighted houses to come home to. How lucky they were, I thought enviously.

Finally, one day we found a furnished apartment on the second floor of a three-story house. The furniture was worn, and the owner's brother walked through our hallway to get to his room in the attic. But there were two bedrooms, and the window to the south looked out on a small garden full of trees.

"We'll take it," we said quickly.

We wrote immediately to our parents, and they soon came by train to join us. Our new apartment was a far cry from our home in Berkeley, but we were together once more, and most important, we were all free. It was a joyous reunion for us in the outside world.

When summer was over, Kay returned to her job at Mt. Holyoke, and I prepared for my first job as a teacher.

Frankford Friends School was established in 1833 and had an enrollment of about one hundred students. The principal was a friendly, motherly woman who taught the fifth and sixth grades and ran an orderly, disciplined school.

Another young woman taught the third and fourth grades, and in the room next to hers, I would teach grades one and two. We had a red school bus that picked up most of the children, and the wife of the driver ran the school cafeteria in the basement.

I could hardly believe I was actually going to be a teacher in a real school and not just an assistant or a temporary teacher in a concentration camp. This was a real job, and I was listed in the school catalog as a member of the faculty with an MEd from Smith College.

Mama and Papa told me how proud they were of me and wished me luck on my first day of school. I knew Mama would have a special celebration dinner waiting for me that evening.

As I set out for Frankford on the elevated train, I was nervous and excited and felt as though everything inside me was jumping up and down.

I arrived at school early to make sure everything was

ready in my classroom. The second-grade desks were arranged neatly to my right, and the first graders would sit around a big table to my left.

I heard the school bus pull into the yard, and a swarm of noisy, laughing children jumped off, scattering quickly to their classrooms.

The bell rang promptly at 9:00, and twenty-four first and second graders rushed into my room scrambling for seats. They smiled as they looked me over, wriggling, giggling, and whispering to each other. They were not so different, I thought, from the children in my classes at Tanforan and Topaz.

I smiled at them then, took a deep breath, and said, "Good morning, boys and girls. My name is Miss Uchida, and I'm going to be your teacher."

EPILOGUE

Changes sometimes come slowly, both for us and for the world.

It was a long time before I understood who I really was. But a trip to Japan on a Ford Foundation Fellowship in 1952 began to turn things around for me. This time I was an adult, doing more than counting bows. I was collecting folk tales that eventually became a part of *The Magic Listening Cap* and *The Sea of Gold*.

This time the blinders were off. I saw Japan in a new light and found the extraordinary beauty and richness of its life and art totally breathtaking.

I traveled throughout Japan and discovered folk art— the art of the people. I found that the simple, honest work of these craftsmen had a wholeness of spirit that spoke to something deep inside me.

I got to know the three men who founded the Folk Art Movement, and translated the poetry of one of them—the master potter, Kanjiro Kawai.

"I am you," he wrote, "The you that only I can see."

He introduced Zen Buddhist thought into my consciousness, drop by drop, in small doses. Sometimes I understood, and sometimes I didn't. But I was growing and reaching, and that felt good.

Slowly, I realized that everything I admired and loved about Japan was a part of me. It always had been. My parents had been giving it to me, like a gift, every day of my life.

In my eagerness to be accepted as an American during my youth, I had been pushing my Japaneseness aside. Now at last, I appreciated it and was proud of it. I had finally come full circle.

Now it was time for me to pass on this sense of pride and self-esteem to the third generation Japanese Americans— the Sansei—and to give them the kinds of books I'd never had as a child. The time was right, for now the world, too, was changing. The civil rights movement and the growth of ethnic pride had touched us all.

I wanted to give the young Sansei a sense of continuity and knowledge of their own remarkable history. I began by writing *Samurai of Gold Hill,* an account of the first Japanese settlers in California. I also wrote about the Japanese American experience in *Journey to Topaz, Journey Home,* and later, *Desert Exile,* to help them understand what their parents and grandparents endured during World War II. That they survived the uprooting was truly a triumph of the human spirit. And I hoped all young Americans would read these books as well.

In the Rinko trilogy, *A Jar of Dreams, The Best Bad Thing,* and *The Happiest Ending,* I hoped to convey the strength of spirit as well as the sense of purpose, hope, and affirmation that sustained the early Japanese immigrant families.

Although these books are not about my own life, I tried to evoke in them the warm sense of family that my mother and father instilled in me, and something of their spirit dwells in Rinko's parents, as it does in many of my fictional parents. There is also a good bit of me in Rinko, although she had more gumption than I did as a child and discovers her self-worth earlier. Just as my own parents encouraged me to follow my dreams, hers, too, help her hold on to hers.

I hope the young people who read these books will dare to have big dreams, as well. I also hope they will learn to see Japanese Americans not in the usual stereotypic way, but as fellow human beings. For although it is important for each of us to cherish our own special heritage, I believe, above everything else, we must all celebrate our common humanity.

There is a footnote to add regarding the wartime uprooting. Some forty years after that tragic event, our country acknowledged at last that it had made a terrible mistake.

In 1976, President Gerald R. Ford stated, "Not only was that evacuation wrong, but Japanese Americans were and are loyal Americans."

In 1982, a commission established by President Jimmy Carter and the United States Congress concluded after an exhaustive inquiry that a grave injustice had been done to Japanese Americans, and that the causes of the uprooting were race prejudice, war hysteria, and a failure of political leadership.

In 1988, a Redress Bill was passed by Congress to mitigate some of the massive financial losses suffered by the Japanese Americans, but it was not put into effect until October 1990. It came too late for most of the Issei who, like my own parents, were gone, and too late for many Nisei as well.

I have written several short stories and books that tell of this wartime uprooting, and each time I find it hard to believe that such a thing actually took place in the United States of America. But it did.

I find it painful to continue remembering and writing about it. But I must. Because I want each new generation of Americans to know what once happened in our democracy. I want them to love and cherish the freedom that can be snatched away so quickly, even by their own country.

Most of all, I ask them to be vigilant, so that such a tragedy will never happen to any group of people in America ever again.

PUBLISHED WORKS

For Young Readers

1949 *The Dancing Kettle,* Harcourt, Brace.*
1951 *New Friends for Susan,* Charles Scribners.
1955 *The Magic Listening Cap,* Harcourt, Brace.*
1957 *The Full Circle,* Friendship Press.
1958 *Takao and Grandfather's Sword,* Harcourt, Brace.
1959 *The Promised Year,* Harcourt, Brace.
1960 *Mik and the Prowler,* Harcourt, Brace.
1962 *Rokubei and the Thousand Rice Bowls,*
       Charles Scribners.
1963 *The Forever Christmas Tree,* Charles Scribners.
1964 *Sumi's Prize,* Charles Scribners.
1965 *The Sea of Gold,* Charles Scribners.*
1966 *Sumi's Special Happening,* Charles Scribners.
1967 *In-Between Miya,* Charles Scribners.

1969 *Sumi and the Goat and the Tokyo Express,*
      Charles Scribners.

1969 *Hisako's Mysteries,* Charles Scribners.

1970 *Makoto, the Smallest Boy,* Thomas Y. Crowell.

1971 *Journey to Topaz,* Charles Scribners.*

1972 *Samurai of Gold Hill,* Charles Scribners.*

1975 *The Birthday Visitor,* Charles Scribners.

1976 *The Rooster Who Understood Japanese,*
      Charles Scribners.

1978 *Journey Home,* Atheneum.
      A Margaret K. McElderry Book.

1981 *A Jar of Dreams,* Atheneum.
      A Margaret K. McElderry Book.

1983 *The Best Bad Thing,* Atheneum.
      A Margaret K. McElderry Book.

1984 *Tabi: Journey Through Time,*
      United Methodist Publishing House.

1985 *The Happiest Ending,* Atheneum.
      A Margaret K. McElderry Book.

1987 *The Two Foolish Cats,*
      Margaret K. McElderry Books.

For Adult Readers

1982 *Desert Exile: The Uprooting of a Japanese American Family,* University of Washington Press.

1987 *Picture Bride* (a novel), Northland Press.

*Currently published by Creative Arts Book Company, Berkeley, CA.

BEST IN BIOGRAPHY AND AUTOBIOGRAPHY FROM BEECH TREE BOOKS

———

ANNE FRANK: LIFE IN HIDING
by Johanna Hurwitz

ANONYMOUSLY YOURS
by Richard Peck

BUT I'LL BE BACK AGAIN
by Cynthia Rylant

DEAR DR. BELL . . . YOUR FRIEND, HELEN KELLER
by Judith St. George

E. B. WHITE: SOME WRITER!
by Beverly Gherman

IN KINDLING FLAME: THE STORY OF HANNAH SENESH, 1921–1944
by Linda Atkinson

THE LIFE AND DEATH OF MARTIN LUTHER KING, JR.
by James Haskins

LOUISA MAY: THE WORLD AND WORKS OF LOUISA MAY ALCOTT
by Norma Johnston

MAKING A DIFFERENCE: THE STORY OF AN AMERICAN FAMILY
by Margaret Hodges

THE ROAD FROM HOME: THE STORY OF AN ARMENIAN GIRL
by David Kherdian